U.S. Supreme Court Transcript of Record Milwaukee Nat Bank of Wisconsin v. City Bank of Oswego

U.S. Supreme Court

U.S. Supreme Court Transcript of Record
Milwaukee Nat Bank of Wisconsin v. City Bank of Oswego

Table of Contents

I. Transcript of Record

TRANSCRIPT OF RECORD.

SUPREME COURT OF THE UNITED STATES.

No. 473.

THE MILWAUKEE NATIONAL BANK, OF WISCONSIN,
PLAINTIFF IN ERROR,

VS.

THE CITY BANK.

IN ERROR TO THE CIRCUIT COURT OF THE UNITED STATES FOR THE
NORTHERN DISTRICT OF NEW YORK.

FILED SEPTEMBER 11, 1878.

SUPREME COURT OF THE UNITED STATES.

No. 473.

THE MILWAUKEE NATIONAL BANK OF WISCONSIN, PLAINTIFF IN ERROR,

VS.

THE CITY BANK.

IN ERROR TO THE CIRCUIT COURT OF THE UNITED STATES FOR THE NORTHERN DISTRICT OF NEW YORK.

INDEX.

	Original.	Print.
Summons	1	1
Order for defendant's appearance	3	1
Complaint	5	1
Answer	21	6
Minutes of trial and verdict	29	8
Order staying proceedings for bill of exceptions	31	9
Judgment	33	9
Bill of exceptions	37	10
Bond on appeal	221	75
Writ of error	225	76
Citation and proof of service	227	76
Clerk's certificate	229	77

1   The President of the United States of America to the marshal of the northern district of New York, greeting :

You are hereby commanded that you summon The City Bank of Oswego to be and appear before the judges of the circuit court of the United States in and for the northern district of New York, in the second circuit, at the City Hall, in the city of Albany, on the second Tuesday of October, A. D. 1875, to answer unto The Milwaukee National Bank of Wisconsin, plaintiff, of a plea of trespass, and also to a bill of complaint of the said plaintiff for forty-two thousand dollars, and interest since September 1, 1869, for the negligent and wrongful misappropriation of a quantity of wheat the property of said plaintiff. And do you then and there make due return of this writ.

Witness the honorable Morrison R. Waite, Chief Justice of the Supreme Court of the United States, at the city of Utica, this 7th day of July, A. D. 1875.

[L. S.]   CHARLES MASON, *Clerk.*

GEORGE G. FRENCH,
    Plaintiff's Attorney, Mexico, N. Y.

2   I certify that on the 2d day of August, 1875, at the city of Oswego, in the county of O'wego, N. Y., in my district, I personally served the within summons on Delos De Wolf, president of the City Bank of Oswego, by showing to him the same, with the seal of the court thereon, and at the same time delivering to and leaving with him a copy thereof.

Dated Oswego, August 2d, 1875.

ISAAC F. QUIMBY,
    U. S. Marshal,
By S. M. TUCKER,
    U. S. Deputy Marshal.

Fees, $13.10.

(Indorsed :) U. S. circuit court, north. dist. of N. Y. The Milwaukee National Bank of Wisconsin vs. The City Bank of Oswego. Summons. Returnable at October term, 1875. Filed Aug. 23, 1875.

3   United States circuit court, northern district of New York, October 11, 1875.

THE MILWAUKEE NATIONAL BANK OF
        Wisconsin
            vs.
    THE CITY BANK.

On filing præcipe in this cause, and on motion of Albertus Perry, ordered that his appearance as attorney for the defendant herein be, and the same is hereby, entered, and that this cause be now docketed for said defendant.

4, 5   Circuit court of the United States in and for the northern district of New York.

THE MILWAUKEE NATIONAL BANK OF
        Wisconsin
            against
    THE CITY BANK.

The complaint of the above named plaintiff, by Geo. G. French, its

REC. 473—1

attorney, respectfully shows and alleges that at the time of the commencement of this suit, and prior thereto, the said plaintiff was, and still is, a banking corporation, created by and organized under the laws of the United States, and located in and having its place of business in the city of Milwaukee, in the State of Wisconsin.

And said plaintiff alleges, on information and belief, that at the time of the commencement of this suit the said defendant was, and had been prior thereto, and still is, a corporation created by and organized under the laws of the State of New York, and having its office and place of business in the city of Oswego, in the State of New York.

And said plaintiff alleges that heretofore, to wit, on or about the 27th day of September, 1869, the said plaintiff discounted for the firm
6   of Mower, Church and Bell, of the city of Milwaukee, two certain drafts drawn by said firm on the firm of A. F. Smith & Co., of ,Oswego, one a sight draft for five thousand and eighty-five dollars and forty-three cents, the other a time draft at thirty days for fifteen thousand dollars, and at the time of the discounting of the said drafts, and in consideration thereof, said Mower, Church and Bell delivered to said plaintiff a bill of lading, duly signed by one John T. Davison, who then was captain of a vessel called the Atwater, and which bill of lading, among other things, recited that said Mower, Church and Bell had shipped in good order and condition on board said vessel, whereof said Davison was master, bound from the port of Milwaukee for the port of Oswego, New York, seventeen thousand bushels number two Milwaukee wheat, and which wheat was to be transported from said port of Milwaukee to said port of Oswego at an agreed freight of thirteen cents per bushel, dangers of fire and navigation excepted, and to be delivered at Oswego for the account of T. L. Baker, the cashier of the plaintiff.

And said plaintiff alleges that the entire quantity of wheat mentioned in the said bill of lading was actually on board of said vessel at
7   the time the said bill of lading was executed, and that said T. L. Baker was, at the time, the cashier of the plaintiff, and acting as such for plaintiff.

And said plaintiff alleges that, after discounting said two drafts drawn by said firm of Mower, Church and Bell upon said A. F. Smith & Co., and the receipt from said firm of Mower, Church and Bell of the said bill of lading, the said plaintiff, by its said cashier, T. L. Baker, enclosed said drafts and bill of lading in a letter, dated at Milwaukee, September 29th, 1869, addressed to D. Mannering, cashier, and who, at the date of the said letter, was the cashier of the said defendant, and in said letter specifically instructed said cashier of said defendant that on payment of the said drafts to deliver the said cargo of wheat to the order of A. F. Smith & Co., and if said drafts were not paid to hold the wheat and advise him (said Baker) by telegraph, and further instructing said cashier that said firm of A. F. Smith & Co. would pay all expenses on said wheat.

And said plaintiff alleges that said D. Mannering, the cashier of said defendant, received the said letter, with the said drafts and bill
8   of lading enclosed, and immediately on receipt thereof presented to the firm of A. F. Smith & Co. the sight draft for payment and the time draft for acceptance, and by letter dated on the 4th day of October, 1869, said cashier of said defendant acknowledged the receipt of said drafts and bill of lading, and advised the remitting of the proceeds of the sight draft, less exchange and commissions retained by said defendant, to the credit of the plaintiff to its corresponding bank in New York City.

And said plaintiff alleges that the said A. F. Smith & Co. paid the sight draft and accepted the said time draft, and returned the said time draft accepted to said cashier of said defendant, who retained the same and the bill of lading.

And said plaintiff alleges that the said schooner Atwater arrived at the port of Oswego with the said wheat on board on the evening of the 8th day of October, 1869, and on the morning of the ninth day of October, 1869, the captain of the said vessel applied to the said cashier of the said defendant for an order for the delivery of the said cargo of
9   wheat, and thereupon the cashier of the said defendant, acting for and on behalf of said defendant, endorsed on the back of the captain's bill of lading an order in these words: " Deliver to the Corn Exchange elevator, for the account of T. L. Baker, cashier, Milwaukee, subject to the order of the City Bank, Oswego, Oct. 9th, 1869. D. Mannering, cash'r."

And said plaintiff alleges that the said cashier of the said defendant did not at the time of the giving of said order to said captain make it a condition in the said order that the said wheat should be so delivered upon the payment of the freight by A. T. Smith & Co.

And said plaintiff alleges that said cashier of said defendant well knew at the time he gave the said order that the said A. F. Smith & Co. were the same parties upon whom the drafts were drawn, and that they were the proprietors of the said Corn Exchange elevator, and well knew that the said cargo of wheat, under and by virtue of said order, would go into the possession of said A. F. Smith & Co. before the payment of said time draft.

And said plaintiff alleges that the captain of said vessel delivered the said cargo of wheat into the said Corn Exchange elevator, but
10   did not, on such delivery, receive payment of the freight from said A. F. Smith & Co.

And said plaintiff alleges that the said A. F. Smith & Co., immediately upon the receipt of said cargo of wheat under said order, sold and shipped the same to divers persons and parties and received money therefor; and said plaintiff alleges, upon information and belief, that the said A. F. Smith & Co. paid the said money so received for said cargo of wheat, or a large portion of the same, to the said defendant, and the said defendant received the said money, knowing that it was the proceeds of the said wheat, and wrongfully applied the proceeds, the said money, as directed by said A. F. Smith & Co., and did not apply the said money or any portion to the payment of the said time draft of said plaintiff.

And said plaintiff alleges that the said defendant well knew of the said shipments and sale of the said cargo of said wheat by said A. F. Smith & Co., and well knew that the money received therefor was paid by said A. F. Smith & Co. to it, said defendant, and, well know-
11   ing these facts, wrongfully took and converted the said money so paid to it by said A. F. Smith & Co. to other purposes than the payment of the said time draft of the said plaintiff.

And said plaintiff alleges that the amount so paid in by said A. F. Smith & Co. to said defendant, out of the proceeds of said sales and shipments of said wheat, exceeds the sum of twenty thousand dollars.

And said plaintiff alleges that said sales and shipments of said wheat were made by said A. F. Smith & Co. with the knowledge, consent, and approval of the said defendant, and in violation of the instructions of this plaintiff to said defendant, and without the knowledge, approval, consent, or sanction of this plaintiff.

And said plaintiff alleges that the said A. F. Smith & Co. did not pay the freight on the said cargo of wheat from Milwaukee to Oswego, and that afterwards a suit was instituted by the owner of such vessel to recover said freight; and said plaintiff was compelled to pay and did pay large sums of money in and about said suit, and was ultimately obliged to pay said freight, and of all which said defendant had due notice.

12

And said plaintiff alleges that by reason of the premises the said plaintiff has lost the said wheat and its proceeds, and has sustained damages to the amount of thirty thousand dollars.

And for a second cause of action said plaintiff alleges that heretofore, to wit, on the 29th day of September, 1869, the said firm of Mower, Church & Bell presented to said plaintiff for discount two drafts drawn by said firm on A. F. Smith & Co., of Oswego, New York, bearing date on said last mentioned day, one a sight draft for four thousand and fifty-two dollars and sixty-two cents, and the other a time draft for seventeen thousand dollars; that said plaintiff discounted said two drafts; that said firm of Mower, Church & Bell, at the time they procured said discount of said drafts, and in consideration of said discount transferred and delivered to said plaintiff a bill of lading signed by one M. M. Holland, who at the time of signing said bill of lading, was a captain of a vessel called the D. G. Fort, and which said bill of lading, among other things, recited that the said firm of Mower, Church & Bell had shipped in good order and condition on board of said schooner D. G. Fort seventeen thousand five hundred and fifty bushels of number one Milwaukee wheat, and which wheat by the terms of the said bill of lading was to be transported from the port of Milwaukee to the said port of Oswego at an agreed price for freight of thirteen cents per bushel, and to deliver the same at Oswego for account of T. L. Baker, cashier, dangers by fire and navigation excepted.

13

And said plaintiff alleges that said wheat was on board of said vessel at the date of the execution of said bill of lading.

And said plaintiff alleges that the said T. L. Baker, named in the said bill of lading, was the cashier of said plaintiff; and the said bill of lading was taken by the said Baker as such cashier, and in no other capacity.

And the said plaintiff alleges that upon discounting the said drafts and receiving said bill of lading, it by its said cashier, T. L. Baker, enclosed the said drafts and bill of lading in a letter addressed to D. Mannering, cashier of said defendant, and in and by which letter said Mannering was specially instructed, that on the wheat going into store in Oswego to have it insured for enough to cover the said drafts, and on payment of the drafts to deliver the cargo named in the bill of lading to the order of A. F. Smith & Co., and if the drafts were not paid to hold the wheat, and advise said plaintiff by telegraph, and further instructing said cashier that A. F. Smith & Co. would pay all expenses.

14

And said plaintiff alleges that the said D. Mannering at the time said letter was written was, and prior thereto had been, and still is the cashier of the said defendant.

And said plaintiff alleges that said letter of instructions, with the enclosed drafts and bill of lading, was received by the said D. Mannering, cashier of the defendant, on or about the 4th day of October, 1869, and on receipt thereof the said cashier presented to A. F. Smith & Co. the sight draft for payment, and the time draft for acceptance; that A. F. Smith & Co. paid the sight draft and accepted the time draft, and

returned the time draft accepted to said cashier of said defendant,
15   who retained the same and the said bill of lading.

And said plaintiff alleges that the said schooner D. G. Fort arrived at the city of Oswego with the said wheat on board on the evening of the 8th of October, 1869, and on the morning of the ninth day of October, 1869, the captain of said schooner applied to the said D. Mannering, cashier of said defendant, for instruction as to the delivery of the said cargo, and thereupon the said Mannering, as cashier of the said defendant, and acting for the said defendant, gave an order to said captain of said vessel to deliver said cargo of wheat to the Corn Exchange elevator for the account of T. L. Baker, cashier, subject to the order of the City Bank of Oswego.

And said plaintiff alleges that the said captain of said vessel, under and by virtue of the said order, delivered said wheat into the Corn Exchange elevator.

And said plaintiff alleges that the said A. F. Smith & Co., at the time the said order was given, and the said cargo of wheat was delivered, were the proprietors of said elevator, and were the same firm upon which said drafts were drawn, and which said fact said defendant
16   well knew at the time said order was given.

And said plaintiff alleges that said A. F. Smith & Co. did not pay the freight on the said cargo.

And said plaintiff alleges that the said A. F. Smith & Co., immediately upon the receipt of said cargo of wheat, sold and shipped the same to divers persons, firms and parties, and received in money the proceeds of said sales and shipments.

And said plaintiff alleges that the said cargo of wheat was thus placed by said defendant in the manual possession of said A. F. Smith & Co., prior to the payment of the time draft, and in violation of the instructions of said plaintiff.

And the said plaintiff alleges, on information and belief, that said defendant, at the time it gave by its cashier said order, well knew that the said A. F. Smith & Co., upon whom the drafts were drawn, were the proprietors of the said Corn Exchange elevator, and said plaintiff alleges that said defendant well knew that said A. F. Smith & Co. were selling and shipping the said cargo of wheat, and converting the same into money.

And said plaintiff alleges that the said A. F. Smith & Co. paid
17   the money the proceeds of the said cargo of wheat to the said defendant, and the said defendant received the said money the proceeds of said sales and shipments of said wheat, and wrongfully applied the said money to its own use, and did not, and would not, and have not applied the said money or any part thereof to the payment of the said time draft of said plaintiff.

And said plaintiff alleges that by the said acts of said defendant the said cargo of wheat and its proceeds has become lost to the said plaintiff.

And said plaintiff alleges that its said time draft is still unpaid.

And said plaintiff alleges that owing to the neglect and failure of the said defendant to make the delivery of said cargo to the Corn Exchange elevator, defendant, upon the payment of the freight by A. F. Smith & Co., this plaintiff, after said wheat had been sold and shipped by said A. F. Smith & Co., and said A. F. Smith & Co. had received the proceeds thereof, and paid the same to said defendant, was obliged to defend a suit brought by the owner of the said vessel to recover the amount of the said freight, and to pay out large sums of money in the
18   costs and expenses of said suit, and of all which said defend-

ant was duly notified, and said plaintiff was ultimately, by reason of the neglect and failure of said defendant to make as a condition of delivery of said wheat the payment of the freight, obliged to pay the said freight, and all the costs and expenses of said suit.

And said plaintiff alleges that by reason of the premises and of the said wrongful acts of said defendant it, said plaintiff, has lost the said cargo of wheat and its proceeds, and has sustained damages to the amount of thirty thousand dollars.

Wherefore said plaintiff demands judgment for the sum of sixty thousand dollars, its damages, and the costs of this suit.

GEO. G. FRENCH,
Pl'ff's Att'y.

19, 20   (Indorsed:) Circuit court United States, northern dist. New York. The Milwaukee National Bank of Wisconsin vs. The City Bank. Complaint. Geo. G. French, pl'ff's att'y.

To A. PERRY, Esq.:

Please take notice of the with' copy complaint.

G. G. FRENCH,
Pl'ff's Att'y.

Filed July 10, 1877.

21   Circuit court of the United States for the northern district of New York.

THE MILWAUKEE NATIONAL BANK OF WIS-
        consin
               vs.
      THE CITY BANK.

The City Bank, the defendant in this action, answers the complaint of the Milwaukee National Bank of Wisconsin, plaintiff herein, as follows:

First. The said defendant, answering the cause of action firstly alleged in said complaint, admits that the plaintiff was and is a banking corporation, created and organized as in said complaint alleged, and located and having its place of business in the city of Milwaukee, in the State of Wisconsin, and also admits that the defendant has been and is a corporation created and organized as is in said complaint alleged, and has its office and place of business in the city of Oswego, in the State of New York.

And said defendant denies the said first alleged cause of action in said complaint contained, and each and every allegation thereof,
22   except as above expressly admitted.

Second. And said defendant, further answering said first alleged cause of action in said complaint, says that at the time of the making of the order for the delivery of the cargo of wheat of the schooner Atwater, in said complaint mentioned and referred to, by David Mannering' the cashier of defendant, to wit, on the ninth day of October, 1869, the said A. F. Smith & Co., in said complaint named, were and for more than one year previous thereto had been, as proprietors of the Corn Exchange elevator in said complaint mentioned, warehouse men of good repute and credit for pecuniary responsibility and moral honesty, and engaged in the business of receiving and storing grain for hire in said Corn Exchange elevator, and the said defendant was not and had never been engaged in the business of storing grain, and had no warehouse or other facilities for so doing, all of which was well known to said plaintiff. And the said Mannering made the said order for the purpose of procuring the said wheat to be stored and taken care of in the said

23   Corn Exchange elevator for the account of said plaintiff and subject to the order of said defendant, and for no other purpose whatever.

Third. The said defendant, answering the cause of action secondly alleged in said complaint, denies the same and each and every allegation therein contained.

Fourth. And said defendant, further answering the cause of action secondly alleged in said complaint, says that at the time of the making of the order for the delivery of the cargo of wheat of the schooner D. G. Fort, in said complaint mentioned and referred to, by David Mannering, the cashier of the defendant, to wit, on the ninth day of October, 1869, the said A. F. Smith & Co. were, and for more than one year previous thereto, had been, as proprietors of the Corn Exchange elevator, mentiond in said complaint, warehouse men of good repute and credit for pecuniary responsibility and moral honesty and engaged in the business of receiving and storing grain for hire in said Corn Exchange elevator, and the said defendant was not and had never been engaged in the bu-

24   siness of storing grain and had no warehouse or other facilities for so doing, all of which was well known to said plaintiff. And said Mannering made the the said order for the purpose of procuring the said wheat to be stored and taken care of in the said Corn Exchange elevator for the account of said plaintiff and subject to the order of said defendant, and for no other purpose whatever.

Fifth. And said defendant, further answering the two causes of action alleged in said complaint, says that before and during the year 1869 it was, has since been, and still is a banking association, organized under and in pursuance of an act of the legislature of the State of New York, entitled "An act to authorize the business of banking," passed April 18, 1838, and the several acts amending the same, and the only powers possessed by said defendant now, or in 1869, are the powers conferred upon it by said acts, to wit, " to carry on the business of banking by discounting bills, notes, and other evidences of debt; by receiving deposits; by buying and selling gold and silver bullion, foreign coins and bills of exchange * * * ; by loaning money on real and personal security; and by exercising such incidental powers as shall be necessary to carry on such business."

25   And said defendant says that it did not in the year 1869 or at any other time have legal power or authority to accept or receive grain or other produce consigned to it to be stored, taken care of, and sold, shipped, or otherwise disposed of, or to promise or undertake for hire or otherwise to receive, store, take care of, or otherwise dispose of grain or other produce consigned to it, and neither the said defendant, nor David Mannering as its cashier, had legal power or authority to accept or receive the cargoes of wheat mentioned in said complaint or to make any orders for the delivery or storage thereof, or to procure the same to be insured, stored, or otherwise disposed of, or to undertake or promise to receive, store, take care of, or otherwise dispose of said wheat, or to become obligated in any way to the plaintiff for the storage, care, or disposition of said wheat.

And said defendant avers that the orders made by said Mannering for the delivery of said wheat and all acts done by him in relation to said wheat, in procuring the same to be insured or otherwise, or in undertaking to store or care for said wheat, were wholly unauthorized

26   and void, and the said defendant is in no way responsible for the acts or omissions of duty (if any) of the said Mannering in respect to the care, custody, or disposition of said wheat.

Sixth. And said defendant, further answering the two causes of action alleged in said complaint, says that before the commencement of this action the said plaintiff, by action at law and otherwise, recovered, collected, and received from the several persons, firms, and parties to whom the said A. F. Smith & Co. sold and shipped the wheat mentioned in said complaint, as therein alleged, the value of the wheat so sold and shipped to said persons, firms, and parties respectively, and thereby obtained and received full payment and satisfaction for their interest and property in the said wheat, for which the said plaintiff seeks to recover in this action.

ALBERTUS PERRY,
Defendant's Attorney.

27, 28   (Indorsed :) Circuit court of U. S., N. dist. of New York. The Milwaukee National Bank of Wisconsin vs. The City Bank. Answer. Albertus Perry, def't's att'y. Filed July 11, 1877.

29   At a stated term of the circuit court of the United States of America for the northern district of New York, in the second circuit, held at the village of Canandaigua on Monday, the 9th day of July, in the year of our Lord one thousand eight hundred and seventy-seven.

Present, the honorable Hoyt H. Wheeler, judge.

Geo. G. French & Mr. Finch.

THE MILWAUKEE NATIONAL BANK OF WIS-
consin
vs.
THE CITY BANK.

A. Perry & F. Kernan.

On motion of George G. French, plaintiff's attorney, ordered that a jury be empannelled, and that the trial of this cause do now proceed.

Whereupon the following-named jurors were called and sworn :

William G. McKelvie.	Hugh A. Gates.	Frederick A. Sackett.
Alexander A. Halsey.	John H. Crandall.	John D. Tricky.
Menzo Coleman.	Ira Clemans.	William Chipps.
Hugh Fulton.	David Wylis.	Albert N. Knapp.

Mr. Finch opens case for plaintiff.
Recess until 2 o'clock p. m.

30   2 o'clock p. m., court met.
Present, Judge Wheeler.

THE MILWAUKEE NATIONAL BANK OF WIS-
consin
vs.
THE CITY BANK.

Jury called; 12 answer; trial proceeds.
Testimony read pursuant to stipulation.
Plaintiff's witness: Delos De Wolf.
Court adjourned until 9½ o'clock a. m. to-morrow.

TUESDAY, *July* 10, 1877.

9½ o'clock a. m., court met.
Present, Judge Wheeler.

SAME)
  vs. }
SAME.)

July called; 12 answer; trial proceeds.
Depositions for plaintiff read.
Plaintiff's witness: Geo. G. French.
Pl'ff rests.
Recess until 2 o'clock p. m.

31   2 o'clock p. m., court met.
Present, Judge Wheeler.

SAME)
  vs. }
SAME.)

Jury called; 12 answer.
Mr. Perry requests court to direct a verdict for the defendant.
Argument pro & con.

WEDNESDAY, *July* 11, 1877.

9½ o'clock a. m., court met.
Present, Judge Wheeler.

THE MILWAUKEE NATIONAL BANK OF WIS-)
            consin   }
              vs.   }
        THE CITY BANK.   )

Jury called; 12 answer.
Court directs the jury to render a verdict for the defendant.
The jury here, under direction of the court, answer and say they find
a verdict for the defendant.
On filing stipulation signed by the attorneys for the respective par-
    ties, Ordered, that the plaintiff have sixty days from this date
32 in which to prepare and serve bill of exceptions in the above en-
    titled cause, and in the mean time and until said expiration of
said sixty days from this date all proceedings on the part of the defendant are stayed. And it is further ordered that if a bill of exceptions is
served the defendant may have thirty days thereafter in which to prepare amendments.

33   United States circuit court, northern district of New York.

THE MILWAUKEE NATIONAL BANK OF WIS-)
            consin   }
              vs.   }
        THE CITY BANK.   )

The issues in this action having been brought on for trial at a term of
said circuit court, held at the court-house in the village of Canandai-

gua, on the 9th, 10th, & 11th days of July, 1877, before the honorable Hoyt H. Wheeler, judge presiding, and a jury, and the said issues having then and there been tried, and a verdict in favor of the defendant and against the plaintiff having been duly rendered by said jury, and all proceeding on the part of the defendant having been stayed for the filing of a bill of exceptions, and a bill of exceptions having been filed, and the costs of the defendant having been taxed at one hundred and one dollars and twenty-four cents:

Now, on motion of Albertus Perry, defendant's attorney, it is ordered and adjudged that the said defendant, The City Bank, do recover

34   of the said plaintiff, The Milwaukee National Bank of Wisconsin, the said sum of one hundred and one dollars and twenty-four cents, for its costs so as aforesaid taxed, and have execution therefor.

Judgment signed this 2d day of January, A. D. 1878.

CHARLES MASON,
Clerk.

35, 36 (Indorsed:) U. S. circuit court, north. dist. of N. Y.   The Milwaukee National Bank of Wisconsin vs. The City Bank. (Copy.) Judgment record. Albertus Perry, def't's att'y. Costs, $101.24. Filed Jan'y 2, 1878, 12 m.

37   United States circuit court, northern district of New York, June term, 1877.

THE MILWAUKEE NATIONAL BANK OF Wis-
        consin
        against
        THE CITY BANK.

Be it remembered, that on the ninth day of July, 1877, this cause being at issue and on the calendar for trial, came on for trial before said court, the honorable Hoyt H. Wheeler sitting as judge thereof, at the courthouse in the village of Canandaigua, in said district, and thereupon came as well the said plaintiff, by G. G. French, esq., its attorney, and the said defendant, by Albertus Perry, esq., its attorney, and said cause being called for trial, and the respective parties announcing themselves ready for trial, a jury of twelve good, true, and lawful men was duly called, sworn and empannelled, and thereupon said plaintiff, to maintain the issues on its part, offered to read in evidence the following stipulated facts, to wit:

38   Circuit court United States, northern district of New York.

THE MILWAUKEE NATIONAL BANK OF WIS-
        consin
        against
        THE CITY BANK.

First. It is stipulated and agreed for the purposes of the trial of this cause that the plaintiff is a corporation as alleged in the declaration. That the firm of Mower, Church & Bell are, and at the time of the giving of the orders to purchase by A. F. Smith & Co., as hereinafter set forth, were commission merchants doing business in the city of Milwaukee, State of Wisconsin.

Second. That on Sept. 22d, 1869, the firm of A. F. Smith & Co. wrote a letter to the firm of Mower, Church & Bell, dated at Oswego, N. Y., in which they say, "We propose that you buy for us a very choice cargo No. 2 wheat, at about 1.13, for our local trade, if freights are no more than twelve cents, and you can draw as before. Please reply by telegraph.

39   Third. That Mower, Church & Bell, on the 24th day of September, 1869, telegraphed to A. F. Smith & Co. as follows: "Letters received two, 2, thirteen, 13, freights 12; have drawn sight," which was received at Oswego at eight o'clock p. m. of the same day.

Fourth. That on the 24th of Sept., 1869, A. F. Smith & Co. sent a telegram from Oswego, addressed to Mower, Church & Bell, as follows: "Telegram received; may draw *forth* sight, balance thirty days, on two cargoes. Answer."

Fifth. On the 25th day of Sept., 1869, A. F. Smith & Co. addressed a letter to Mower, Church & Bell, in which, after stating the two last telegrams. they say. " We have your reply; have bought one cargo at limit; will buy another as soon as possible. We are not modest at asking our western friends to draw some portion time, but will try and pay sight on their consignments, unless we all get into a jangle on monetary matters this fall."

Sixth. Sept. 29th, 1869, Mower, Church & Bell telegraphed to A. F. Smith & Co. as follows: "Bought one, 1, cargo at limit;" which was received at Oswego on the same day, at 11.55 a. m.

Seventh. Sept. 25th, 1869. Mower, Church & Bell telegraphed to A.
        F. Smith & Co. as follows: " Freights firm, 13; shall we fill sec-
40   ond (2) cargo? Answer quick." Received at Oswego 5.10 p. m.
        Eighth. Telegram from A. F. Smith & Co. to Mower, Church & Bell, Sept. 28th, as follows: " Not unless price of wheat declines correspondent with advance in freight."

Ninth. Telegram from Mower, Church & Bell to A. F. Smith & Co., dated Sept. 28th, 1869, in these words: " Load Atwater sixteen thousand, (16,000); have bought eight thousand, (8,000,) second, (2,) Chicago."

Tenth. A letter from Mower, Church and Bell to A. F. Smith & Co., as follows:

[Mower, Church & Bell, general commission merchants and shippers. Office, Milwaukee National Bank building; storehouse, 159 W. Water street.]

MILWAUKEE, *Sept.* 25, 1869.

A. F. SMITH & CO.,
    Oswego, N. Y.:

GENTLEMEN: We have bought for you to-day 19,000 No. two, 1.13, and 5,000 No. 2 at 1.12½, making 24,000 in all. We should have bought more, but we had contracted freight, as we supposed, for a 12,000 vessel (at 12 cents), but it seems there was a misunderstanding about it, and we lost the vessel. The best we could do this afternoon, on freight,
        was 13 cts. to Oswego. We have chartered the S. T. Atwater
41   (to) carry 16,000 bush. at that price. We now have 8,000 bush.
        on second cargo. This p. m. we telegraphed you, " Freights firm at thirteen (13); shall we fill the second cargo?" We telegraphed you this evening, "Load Atwater sixteen thousand (16,000); have bought eight thousand (8,000) on second cargo." Market this evening firm at 1.13¼. Wht. No. two quite scarce.

        Yours, truly,
        (Signed)   MOWER, CHURCH & BELL.

Eleventh. A letter from A. F. Smith & Co. to Mower, Church & Bell, as follows:

[Mower, Church & Bell, general commission merchants and shippers. Office, Milwaukee National Bank Building. Storehouse, 159 W. Water street.]

MILWAUKEE, *Sept.* 30, 1869.

A. F. SMITH & CO.:

GENTLEMEN : Yours of the 27th is rec'd, and in reply would say that the eight thousand (8,000) was sold without loss to you, and no loss to us but the commissions. When we bought we were at work on the two cargoes ordered, and supposed the freight was all arranged at 12 cts. ; but it proved otherwise, as we explained, so we sold the surplus. When the vessel came to load, she required one thousand more, which we bought in as reported yesterday, (a) 111½; to-day we enclose acc't

47   purchase for cargo D. G. Fort ; on loading, she required 550 bush. more, which we bought in at 113½ this morning. She sailed this morning. As to the future wheat we hardly know what to say, as prices are now lower than we anticipated, but the unprecedented commotion in N. York, caused by the gold operation, has unsettled our monetary affairs to such an extent that we hardly know what to look for. The season is now well advanced, and our farmers have not been able to thrash much of their crop, and now the price is so low that they are not anxious to market their grain, so we look for not very large receipts this fall. The season for an advance in freight and insurance is at hand, and without a material advance east we much look for lower prices here, which must check our receipts. As to an eastern advance, you are better posted than we are. We think the foreign demand will control prices at the east almost entirely. We had placed considerable reliance on their necessities, but may be mistaken. Our own crop, when fully marketed, will fall considerably short of the estimate, but that will not produce any effect until near another harvest; the weather has been very bad in Minnesota, and considerable of the wheat

48   in the stack is damaged. In looking over the whole ground we come to the conclusion that the price is relatively small, and think the probabilities are that the present price must be sustained.

Hoping to hear from you your views of the prospects of the markets,

We remain yours, with respect,

(Signed)   MOWER, CHURCH & BELL.

Twentieth. A letter from A. F. Smith & Co. to Mower, Church & Bell, as follows:

[Office of A. F. Smith & Co., proprietors of the Corn Exchange elevator, commission merchants for the sale of all kinds of State, Western and Canada grain.]

OSWEGO, N. Y., *Oct.* 4, 1869.

Messrs. MOWER, CHURCH & BELL,
        Milwaukee, Wis. :

GENTLEMEN : Your favors 29th and 30th ult. with enclosures are at hand, and we fully note contents. We find the ac. all right, except in the matter of exchange ; you charge ¾ on whole am't, s't and time, while the exchange on the sight should be only ⅜. Are we correct? The difference, as we make it, is, on Atwater cargo, $19.06 ; on Forts, $15.40. Please advise in regard to this. We are without any

49   opinion as to the future of wheat. Having expressed erroneous ones so frequently, we don't dare venture another in the present state of affairs. Wheat, at present price, does look cheap to us, however.

Yours truly,

(Signed)   A. F. SMITH & CO.

To the reading of all of which from paragraph second to this point said defendant did then and there object as irrelevant and incompetent. Objection sustained and the same was excluded, and to which ruling plaintiff did then and there except.

Said plaintiff then read the following facts, as stipulated, to wit:

Twenty-first. Invoice of the cargo of the Atwater, as follows:

EXHIBIT A. & F., No. 22, A. B. G.

Account purchase of 17,000 bus. No. two (2) wh't by Mower, Church & Bell, Milwaukee, Wis., for account & risk of A. F. Smith & Co., Oswego. N. Y., shipped per sch'r Atwater.

1869.

Sep. 27. 11,000 bus. No. 2 sp. wheat, 113		12,430 00
" " 3,000 " " " " 112½		3,375 00
" " 2,000 " " " " 112¼		2,245 00
" 28. 1,000 " " " " 111½		1,115 00
Sep. 28. Storage on 17,000 bus. of wheat, at 2c		340 00
50 Sep. 28. Marine insurance		106 25
" " Inspection, 30c		5 10
Sep. 28. Weighing, 30c		5 10
" " Commissions		170
" " Stamps on time draft, $15,000		7 50
" " Discount " " " 30 days		137 48
" " Exchange on drafts, ¾		150 35
		$20,086 78

Credits:

Sep. 8. By error in cargo sch'r Phalarope		1 35
" 27. " draft 30 days		15,000 00
" 29. " " sight		5,085 43
		$20,086 78

E. & O. E.

(Signed)   MOWER, CHURCH & BELL.

H.

Twenty-second. Invoice of cargo of D. G. Fort, as follows:

Account purchase of 17,550 bus. No. one (1) wheat by Mower, Church & Bell, Milwaukee, Wis., for account and risk of A. F. Smith & Co., Oswego, N. Y., shipped per sch'r Dan'l G. Fort.

1869.

Sept. 29. To 17,000 bushels No. one (1) wheat, at 114½		19,465 00
" 30. " 550 " " " " " " 113¼		624 25
" 30. To storage on 17,550 bus. wheat at 2c		351 00
Sept. 30. To inspection " " " " 30c		5 25
51 Sept. 30. To commission " " " 1c		175 50
" 29. " discount on $17,000 draft, at 30 days		155 82
Sept. 29. To stamps		8 50
" 30. " exchange, 3¼ per c't		157 66
" " " marine insurance		109 64
		$21,052 62

Credits:

Sept. 29. By draft, 30 days............................. 17,000 00

   " " " "   sight.............................. 4,052 62

                                     $21,052 62

E. & O. E.

(Signed)   MOWER, CHURCH & BELL.

                                    H.

Twenty-third. That Mower, Church & Bell purchased the said wheat in said two invoices mentioned at the dates stated thereon and paid for the same with their own money. That the wheat was delivered on board of the said schooner Atwater and D. G. Fort, at Milwaukee, Wisconsin, and they forthwith sent a duplicate copy of such invoice by mail to A. F. Smith & Co., who received the same several days before the arrival of said wheat at Oswego, and thereupon the captain of said schooner delivered to Mower, Church & Bell bills of lading as follows:

1st. Bill of lading of the Atwater, as follows:

No.   MILWAUKEE, *Sept. 28th,* 1869.

52   Shipped in good order and condition, by Mower, Church & Bell, as agents and forwarders, for account and at the risk of whom it may concern, on board the schooner Atwater, whereof J. T. Davison is master, bound from this port for Oswego, N. Y., the following articles as here marked and described, to be delivered in like good order and condition, as addressed in the margin, or to his or their assigns or consignees, upon paying the freight or charges, as noted below (dangers of navigation, fire, and collision excepted). And it is agreed between the carriers and shippers and assigns that, in consideration especially of the rate of freight herein named, the said carriers, having supervised the weighing of said cargo inboard, hereby agree that this bill of lading shall be conclusive, as between shippers and assigns and carriers, as to the quantity of cargo to be delivered to consignees at the port of destination (except when grain is heated or heats in transit), and that they will deliver the full quantity hereon named, or pay for any part of cargo not delivered, at the current market price; the value thereof to be deducted from the freight money by con-

53   signees, if they shall so elect, and thereupon the carriers shall be subrogated to the shippers' and owners' rights of property and action therefor, and said shippers or owners hereby assign their claim and right of action for such deficiency or deficiencies to the carrier.

In witness whereof, the said master of said vessel hath affirmed to bills of lading, of this tenor and date, one of which being accomplished, the others to stand void.

         Ac. T. L. Baker to City Bank, Oswego, N. Y.

(17,000) seventeen thousand bushels No. two (2) Milwaukee wheat; lake freight thirteen (13) cents per bushel to Oswego.

                        JNO. T. DAVISON.

2d. Bill of lading of the D. G. Fort, as follows:

          Jos. Colt, special commissioner.

No.   MILWAUKEE, *Sept.* 29, 1869.

Shipped in good order and condition, by Mower, Church & Bell, as agents and forwarders, for account and at the risk of whom it may concern, on board the sch'r D. G. Fort, whereof   Holland is master, bound from this port for Oswego, N. Y., the following articles as here 54   marked and described, to be delivered in like good order and condition, as addressed on the margin or to his or their assigns or consignees, upon paying the freight and charges as noted below (dangers of navigation, fire and collision excepted).

And it is agreed between the carriers and shippers and assigns, that, in consideration especially of the rate of freight hereon named, the said carriers, having supervised the weighing of said cargo inboard, hereby agree that this bill of lading shall be conclusive as between shippers and assigns and carriers, as to the quantity of cargo to be delivered to consignees at the port of destination (except when grain is heated or heats in transit), and that they will deliver the full quantity hereon named, or pay for any part of cargo not delivered, at the current market price; the value thereof to be deducted from the freight money by consignees, if they shall so elect, and thereupon the carriers shall be subrogated to the shippers' and owners' rights of property and action therefor.

And said shippers or owners hereby assign their claim and right of action for such deficiency or deficiencies to the carrier.

In witness whereof, the said master of said vessel hath affirmed 55   to   bills of lading of this tenor and date, one of which being accomplished, the other to stand void.

Ac. T. L. Baker to City Bank, Oswego, N. Y.

Seventeen thousand five hundred and fifty bushels (17,550) No. one (1) Milwaukee wheat.

Lake freight, thirteen (13) cents per bushel to Oswego.
                                                    M. M. HOLLAND.

Twenty-fourth. That on the receipt of the said bills of lading of the Atwater, the firm of Mower, Church & Bell drew two drafts on A. F. Smith & Co., of Oswego, dated:

One on the 27th day of Sept., 1869, at thirty days, for.. $15,000 00
The other a sight draft for............................   5,085 43
                                                        _____
                                                          20,085 43

payable to the order of T. L. Baker, cashier, value received; addressed to A. F. Smith & Co., Oswego, N. Y.

Twenty-fifth. That on the receipt of the bill of lading of the cargo of the D. G. Fort, Mower, Church & Bell drew two drafts on A. F. Smith & Co., of Oswego, dated Sept., 29, 1869 :

One at thirty (30) days for........................... $17,000 00
And one at sight for..................................   4,052 62

Twenty-sixth. That Mower, Church & Bell presented the drafts attached to said bills of lading to the plaintiff, at Milwaukee, Wisconsin, for discount, and that said plaintiff discounted said drafts 56   in the usual course of business upon the faith and credit of said bills of lading. That said cargoes were insured for Mower, Church & Bell, and the policies transferred by them to the plaintiff. That said insurance was paid by Mower, Church & Bell and charged in the invoice sent to A. F. Smith & Co.

Twenty-seventh. That said plaintiff, after discounting said drafts, transmitted them, with certificates of insurance, in letters addressed to the City Bank of Oswego, N. Y., as follows:

1st. A letter from T. L. Baker, cashier of the plaintiff, enclosing the drafts and bills of lading of the schooner Atwater to D. Mannering, cashier of the City Bank of Oswego, as follows:

MILWAUKEE, *Sept. 29th*, 1869.

D. MANNERING, Esq, *Cash'r*:

DEAR SIR: I inclose for collection and remittance to Nat. Park Bank, N. Y., bills as stated below. Your favor of   , with enclosures, received:

A. F. Smith & Co., sight $5, 085 43
" "   "   "   30 Oct 15, 000 00

57   B. L. schooner Atwater, 17,000 bushels wheat; in Ætna Ins. Co., 11,250; Home Insurance Co., 10,000; cer., weight and inspection. Please hold above certifs. insurance for arrival of vessel, and on the wheat going into shore please have it insured for enough to cover draft. On payment of the drafts you will please deliver the cargo to order of Messrs. Smith & Co. If not paid, please hold, and advise me by telegraph. Messrs. Smith & Co. will pay all expenses.

Truly, yours,

T. L. BAKER, *Cash'r*.

That said drafts were endorsed on the back thereof as follows:

Pay D. Mannering, cash., or order, for collection on acc'ts of Milwaukee Nat. Bk. of Wis.

T. L. BAKER, *Cashier*.

Twenty-eighth. A letter from T. L. Baker, cashier of the plaintiff, enclosing the drafts and bill of lading and certificates of insurance of schooner D. G. Fort to D. Mannering, cashier of the City Bank of Oswego, as follows:

MILWAUKEE, *Sept. 30th*, 1869.

D. MANNERING, Esq., *Cas.*:

DEAR SIR: I enclose for collection and remittance to Nat. Park Bank, N. Y., bills as stated below.

58   Your favor of   , with enclosures, received. The instructions given you yesterday and on all the cargoes shipped to you for Messrs. A. F. Smith & Co. you will please apply to this.

Truly, yours,

T. L. BAKER, *Cas.*

A. F. Smith & Co., sight 4, 052 62
"   "   "   1 Nov.......................... 17, 000 00

B. L. sch'r D. G. Fort, 17,550 bushels No. 1 wheat. Certf. weight and inspection. Certf. Northwestern Nat. Ins. Co., 21,938.

Twenty-ninth. A letter from D. Mannering, cashier, as follows:

OSWEGO, N. Y., *Oct. 4th*, 1869.

T. L. BAKER, Esq., *Cashier*:

DEAR SIR: Your favor of the 29th inst, with stated enclosure, received.

Yours, respectfully,

D. MANNERING,
Cashier.

I have remitted to the National Bank, New York, for your credit 5,066 36

Ex 19 07

In payment Smith, 5,085.40.

We prefer, after this, not to receive B. L. when we have to look after the property.

A letter from D. Mannering, cashier, as follows:

59　　　　　　　　　　　　　　　　　　　THE CITY BANK,
　　　　　　　　　　　　　　　　Oswego, N. Y., Oct. 7th, 1869.

T. L. BAKER, Esq., *Cashier :*

DEAR SIR: Your favor of the 30th inst. with stated enclosure received.

　　　　　Yours respectfully,

　　　　　　　　　　　　　　　　　D. MANNERING,
　　　　　　　　　　　　　　　　　　　　　Cashier.

I enclose to have remitted to the Nat. Park Bank for your credit $4,037 43

　　　　　　　　　　　　　　　　　　　　　　　　　　15 19

Payment Smith & Co... 4,052 62

Thirtieth. A letter from T. L. Baker to D. Mannering, as follows:

　　　　　　　　　　　　　　　　　　MILWAUKEE, *Oct. 6th,* 1869.

D. MANNERING, Esq., *Cash'r :*

DEAR SIR: I enclose for collection and　　　bills as stated below. Your favor of 4 with enclosures is received and note remarks.

We take very few time cargoes. I would not take any unless we can hold the property. These cargoes were shipped to your bank at the request of Messrs. Smith & Co., and as you wrote me you charged extra for remitting, I suppose it was for the attention and care requisite. The usual rate for remitting from Oswego is $\frac{1}{10}$ c.; on this sight bill

60　you have charged $\frac{3}{4}$. On 30th ult. I shipped you another cargo that I trust will receive your attention. I shall take no more time cargoes, and in future will not ask you to look after the property on arrival.

　　　　　Truly yours,

　　　　　　　　　　　　　　　　　T. L. BAKER, *Cas.*

That said drafts were endorsed on the back thereof as follows: "Pay D. Mannering, cashier, or order, for collection on account of Milwaukee National B'k of Wisconsin."

Thirty-first. That the cashier, D. Mannering, on receipt of said drafts and bills of lading, presented the drafts to A. F. Smith & Co., the sights drafts for payment and the time drafts for acceptance; that A. F. Smith & Co. paid the sight drafts and accepted the time drafts; that the City Bank of Oswego retained in its possession and never delivered said bill of lading to said A. F. Smith & Co.

Thirty-second. That the said schooner Atwater left the city of Milwaukee, Wisconsin, with the said wheat on board and arrived at Oswego, New York, on the evening of the eighth, and on the ninth (9th) day of October, 1869. The captain of said schooner applied to

61　said D. Mannering, cashier, for an order of delivery of said cargo, and thereupon said D. Mannering endorsed on the captain's bill of lading an order in these words: " Deliver to the Corn Exchange elevator for the account of T. L. Baker, cashier, Milwaukee, subject to the order of the City Bank. Oswego, Oct. 9th, 1869. D. Mannering, cash'r." That the captain of said schooner delivered said cargo under said order and took a receipt therefor on the back of the bill of lading on which said order was written, and which receipt was signed in the name of A. F. Smith & Co. by the bookkeeper of said firm, Mr. Forsyth.

Thirty-third. That the said schooner, D. G. Fort, left the city of Milwaukee, Wisconsin, with the said wheat on board and arrived at Oswego on the evening of the 8th of October, and on the 9th day of October, 1869, the captain of said schooner applied to the said D. Mannering, cashier, for an order of delivery of the said cargo, and thereupon the said D. Mannering indorsed on the captain's bill of lading an order in these words: " Deliver to the Corn Exchange elevator for the account of Milwaukee National Bank, subject to the order of the City Bank, Oswego. Oct. 9th, 1869. D. Mannering, cash." That the captain of 62 said schooner delivered said wheat under said order and took a receipt therefor on the back of the said bill of lading on which said order was written, and which receipt was signed in the name of A. F. Smith & Co. by the said bookkeeper of said firm.

Thirty-fourth. That on the receipt of the said cargoes, A. F. Smith & Co. entered the same on their books to their own account. That at the time of the delivery of said cargoes they were the sole lessees of the Corn Exchange elevator. That said elevator is situated on Oswego River, and is used for storage of grain and the transhipment of grain, and has a storage capacity of 250,000 bushels. That at the time the said wheat was delivered said D. Mannering applied to A. F. Smith & Co. for insurance thereon and received a certificate delivered by A. F. Smith & Co., in the following form :

A. F. Smith & Co.

$5,000.

On grain, their own, or held by them on commission, or sold but not delivered ; contained in the Corn Exchange elevator, situated on block No. 63, second ward, Oswego, N. Y. Loss, if any, payable to the City Bank, Oswego, N. Y.

National Ins. Co., Boston, Mass.	$2,500
63 Putman Ins. Co., Hartford, Conn	2,500
For fifteen days from date	$5,000

Oswego. Oct. 4th, 1869.
For above ins. co.'s,

W. NEWKIRK, Ag't.

And the premium and cost of said insurance were paid by said A. F. Smith & Co.

Thirty-fifth. That thereupon, to wit, on said ninth (9) day of October, 1869, the firm of Randall & Kenyon, who were merchants, dealers, and forwarders in grain, purchased in good faith of A. F. Smith & Co. 7,700 bushels of the wheat of the cargo of the schooner Atwater, and 7,400 bushels of the wheat of the cargo of the schooner D. G. Fort. That A. F. Smith & Co., by the direction of Randall & Kenyon as purchasers of the same, shipped the 7,700 bushels into the canal-boat A. Post, and by the like direction shipped the 7,400 into the canal-boat P. B. Davis; that said shipments were made on the ninth day of October, 1869; that bills of lading were signed by the respective captains of said canal-boats reciting that Randall & Kenyon were the shippers; that Randall and Kenyon drew drafts on Hughes, Hickcox & Co. (and consigned the wheat in the canal-boat A. Post) to the amount of $8,085.00 to Hughes, Hickcox & Co. with said canal-boat bill of lading attached, and that said Hughes, Hickcox & Co. paid said draft in the due and usual course of business upon the faith and credit of said bill of lading, and also drew a draft on the wheat in the canal-boat P. B. Davis to the amount of $8,140.00 on Hughes, Hickcox & Co. with said canal-boat bill of lading attached and consigned the same to said Hughes, Hickcox & Co., and that said Hughes, Hickcox & Co. paid said draft in the due and usual course of business upon the faith and credit of said bill of lading.

Thirty-sixth. That said canal-boats and each of them arrived in the city of New York on the fifth day of November, 1869, and the said wheat was delivered to Hughes, Hickcox & Co.

Thirty-seventh. That a demand was made by the plaintiff on that day for said wheat; that said Hughes, Hickcox & Co. refused to deliver said wheat on said demand unless the plaintiffs would make repayment for their said advances as herein recited; that said plaintiffs refused to make such repayments, whereupon Hughes, Hickcox & Co. sold said wheat on the said fifth day of November, 1869, and realized therefor as follows:

7,700 bushels on canal-boat A. Post, 1.30 per bushel.

They paid freight from Oswego	1,540 00
Towing	14 00
Weighing	57 75
Gov't tax	10 03
Commission	150 52
	$1,772 30

7,400 bushels on canal-boat P. B. Davis, at $1.35 per bushel.

They paid freight from Oswego	$1,480 00
Towing	14 00
Weighing	55 50
Gov't tax	10 08
Commission	151 20
	$1,710 78

Thirty-eighth. That the advances made by said Hughes, Hickcox & Co. to Randall & Kenyon were twenty-six days before the arrival of said wheat in the city of New York, and fourteen days before said Hughes, Hickcox & Co. had any notice of any claim whatever to said wheat by the plaintiffs, and in the due and usual course of business, and that said Hughes, Hickcox & Co. at the time of making said advances on such wheat believed that Randall & Kenyon were the true, actual, and bona fide owners thereof.

Fortieth. That the following four letters passed between the firm of A. F. Smith & Co. and Mower, Church & Bell, but do not relate to the wheat in question.

1st. A letter from A. F. Smith & Co. to Mower, Church and Bell, as follows:

[Office of A. F. Smith & Co., proprietors of the Corn Exchange Elevator, commission merchants for the sale of all kinds of State, Western, and Canada grain.]

OSWEGO, N. Y., *Sept.* 1, 1869.

Messrs. MOWER, CHURCH & BELL,
    Milwaukee, Wis.:

GENTS: Yours of the 28th at hand and noted. We shall do something with you again soon for our customers and ourselves, for local trade, as we shall need some very soon again—in fact, before the new wheat moves much, or is fit to grind. But should we do so, your banks must not put such iron-clad instructions to their corresponding bank here. You will do well to inquire about that. This grain for local goes to country millers and give little time, and make 5 to 10c. more per bushel here; we ask time, but your banks say in their instructions to hold the

67   property, and as soon as *as* certain draft is paid, they may deliver grain enough to amount to that. Of course, this is not what we want, for we are ready to pay sight on consignments, and what we order for sale for our customers in large quantities or for furtherance to New York, if all of the trouble can be avoided, which we might have had on the last purchase you made and shipped, and drew time, had our banks lived up to your banks' instructions. We may give you an order again soon. Let us hear from you. Keep us posted.

    Very truly,

                    A. F. SMITH & CO.

(Copy.)

2d. A letter to A. F. Smith & Co. from Mower, Church & Bell, as follows:

MILWAUKEE, *Sept.* 7, 1869.

Messrs. A. F. SMITH & CO.,
    Oswego, N. Y.:

DEAR SIRS: Your telegraphic order, "Buy and ship us load prime No. 1 wheat, draw same time as before, City Bank, load Cortez or Camanche, if there and ready," was received too late last evening to see bankers and learn if they would take time paper: the crop just commencing to move, and don't like to handle it. We succeeded in making

68   the arrangement this a. m. and purchased cargo 16,258$\frac{35}{100}$, at 132$\frac{1}{4}$ and 132 as per enclosed ac. purchase. We have made our time draft 30 and 45 days and sight draft for $3,470.90, which we think will be entirely satisfactory. As regards the bank instructions, which you call iron clad, they decline to vary, and as the time paper was an accommodation, we could hardly in conscience say no. Doubtless you can get the same latitude at your bank as you had upon last time cargo. Market was rated dull and lower to-day, and we believe that when the wheat commences to move lively and the new wheat is solely handled, we shall have lower prices and safer to handle. Wheat would commence to move plentifully till the last third of this month. We send samples of your cargo, sch'r Phalarope, per express; a nice cargo. Hope to hear from you again; ac. enclosed.

    Yours, truly,
(S'g'd)   MOWER, CHURCH & BELL.

3d. A letter from A. F. Smith & Co. to Mower, Church & Bell, as follows:

OSWEGO, N. Y., *Sept.* 14, 1869.

Messrs. MOWER, CHURCH & BELL,
            Milwaukee, Wis.:

      GENTLEMEN : Your favors 7th, 8th and 11th are at hand and
69   contents noted. Your drafts are also in and duly honored. We
cannot but think that your bank is over particular in its instructions to its correspondents here ; more so, in fact, than any other in
your city with which we have had dealings, and somewhat unnecessarily so. However, we can doubtless get along as well as before, as we
ask no favors not bestowed upon others. We agree with you in regard
to wheat. It would seem impossible to keep prices up when the move-
ments of the new crop becomes general, unless foreign m'k'ts should go
higher.

      Yours, truly,

                   A. F. SMITH & CO.

      4th. A letter from Mower, Church & Bell to A. F. Smith & Co., as
follows :

                   MILWAUKEE, *Sept.* 20, 1869.

Messrs. A. F. SMITH & Co.,
            Oswego, N. Y.:

DEAR SIRS : Your letter of the 14th inst. received ; as regards the
instructions given by our bank to their correspondents in regard to
their cargoes, we do not understand that they are any more stringent
        than the other banks here. We spoke of the matter to our banker,
70   who, having inquired, says that he has not exceeded the univer-
        sal rule here ; upon the contrary, thinks he has been within it.
It is our wish that your accommodations shall be as favorable as any
one gets from this city, and we think you are not confined on their time
cargoes more than others. The market continues to decline, although
the shipments are considerable in excess of our receipts. The decline
in No. 1 have not kept pace with other grades, as the demand for
shipment has been principally for No. 1. The recent wet weather has
rather retarded the thrashing in many sections, and the grain is not
moving as universally as it would had we had dry, even weather. We
hope we may hear from you ere long with another substantial order.

      Yours, very truly,
      (S'g)   MOWER, CHURCH & BELL.

      Forty-first. That the cashier of the City Bank of Oswego testifies as
follows : That the bill of lading of the Atwater and D. G. Fort were in
the custody and possession of the City Bank of Oswego, except when
the drafts were sent over for acceptance and payment. That the bills
of lading are sent over with the drafts and all the papers that came
        with them, such as certificates of weight and inspection, certifi-
71   cates of insurance for acceptance of time draft and payment of
        sight draft, and they are returned and kept by the bank, and
when time drafts are paid then the bills of lading and certificates are
given up, if called for, and that no orders were given by the said bank
to A. F. Smith & Co. for the delivery of the said cargoes. If the drafts
are protested the papers all go back to the bank we have received
them from. That the reputation of A. F. Smith & Co. as warehouse
men and merchants in the city of Oswego at the date of the giving of
the orders to the captains of the Atwater and the Fort was good ; that
they stood high as men of integrity.

Forty-second. That A. F. Smith & Co. did not pay the time drafts or either of them; and that they were remitted by the City Bank of Oswago to the plaintiff, together with the bills of lading of the Atwater and the Fort, and that said drafts with the bills of lading are now in possession of the plaintiff.

Thirty-ninth. On the eighteenth day of October, 1869, the City Bank, Oswego, telegraphed to the plaintiff as follows: "A. F. Smith & Co. have failed. You better come here and look after your wheat.

72

On the eighteenth day of October, the plaintiff telegraphed to the defendant as follows: "Do not deliver any wheat to Smith & Co.; will leave to-night."

On the same day, October eigteenth, the plaintiff wrote and sent the following letter to the defendant:

MILWAUKEE, *Oct.* 18, 1869.

D. MANNERING, Esq., Cas.:

DEAR SIR: Your telegraph of this morning announcing the failure of A. F. Smith & Co. was duly received. T. S. Hayden, who is in the employ of the bank, leaves this afternoon for Oswego. I have given him letter to you. He is fully authorized to act for this bank; any assistance given him will be duly appreciated.

Truly, yours,

T. L. BAKER, *Cas.*

The following letter written by plaintiff to defendant was delivered to defendant by T. S. Hayden:

MILWAUKEE, *Oct.* 18, 1869.

D. MANNERING, Esq., Cas.:

73 D'R SIR: Permit me to introduce T. S. Hayden, esq., who visits Oswego to attend to the disposition of wheat held by you for us, viz:

Ex. Schooner Phalarope		8,129	bushels	1	wheat.
" " Atwater		17,000	"	2	"
" " D. G. Fort		17,550	"	1	"

You will please deliver all the wheat to him and the following acceptances of A. F. Smith & Co., viz:-

One due 25 Oct.	9,500
" " 30 "	15,000
" " 1 Nov.	17,000

Mr. Hayden is fully authorized to make all arrangements and settlements and to sign for this bank.

Truly yours,

T. L. BAKER, *Cas.*

On the nineteenth day of October, the plaintiff telegraphed to the defendant as follows: "Do you hold wheat shipped to your care or delivered to consignee?" This telegram was received by the defendant in the morning of October twentieth, and on the same morning the defendant replied by telegraph as follows: "We stored the wheat for your account, subject to our order; we cannot find it."

On receipt of defendant's telegram of October eighteenth above
74   mentioned the plaintiff sent an agent (T. S. Hayden) to Oswego
to find said wheat. That said agent found said wheat, and on
the twenty-second day of October, at 4.17 p. m. telegraphed from Oswego to Hughes, Hickcox & Co., as follows: "Seventy-seven (77) hundred bushels wheat shipped to you from Oswego, October 10, eighteen
hundred and sixty-nine (1869), on canal-boat Alanson Post, and seventy-
four (74) hundred bushels wheat shipped to you on the same day from
Oswego on canal-boat P. B. Davis, is the property of the Milwaukee
National Bank of Wisconsin, which will hold you responsible for the
same." Signed in the name of the cashier of said plaintiff. That said
Hughes Hickcox & Co. received said telegram on the same day in the
city of New York.

Forty-third. Sidney Bickford, who with Ananias F. Smith composed
the firm of A. F. Smith & Co., testifies as follows:

Question. Did the firm of F. Smith & Co. receive grain into the Corn
Exchange elevator simply for storage?

Answer. Yes, sir.

Q. Was the elevator used also simply for the transshipping of
grain?

75   A. It was.

Q. Was the Corn Exchange elevator connected with what was
known as the Oswego Warehouse Association?

A. It was during a portion of October, 1869; the association, I think,
was not formed until about the middle of October, and the Corn Exchange elevator has been connected with that association since it was
organized.

Q. Was it entered in that association as a warehouse for receiving
grain for storage or transhipment?

A. I suppose so.

Q. Was that organization for the purpose of regulating the price or
charges for storage and transhipment?

A. It was.

Q. Was the Corn Exchange elevator known as a public warehouse for
the receipt of grain for storage or transhipment?

A. It was known as a warehouse for that purpose; yes, sir.

Q. What proportion or about what proportion of the whole grain
which was received into that warehouse or shipped therefrom during
the years 1868 and 1869, until Nov., 1869, went into the elevator, either
for storage or transhipment?

76   A. All that went through the elevator went into it for storage
or transhipment.

Q. Were A. F. Smith & Co., advised of any special directions or instructions accompanying bills lading sent to the City Bank of Oswego?

A. Not to my knowledge.

Q. Did A. F. Smith & Co. ever authorize or assent to any instructions
from the plaintiffs, or any of the plaintiffs, to the Merchants' Bank of
Watertown, or the City Bank of Oswego, to withhold the delivery of the
wheat, or any cargo of it, until the payment of the time drafts, or any
instructions to that effect?

A. No, sir.

Q. Were A. F. Smith & Co. called upon for or did they give any warehouse receipts for any of these cargoes?

A. No, sir.

Q. At the time of the payment of the sight draft, and the acceptance
of the time drafts of each or either of these cargoes, did A. F. Smith &

Co. make any express or special arrangement respecting the holding or disposition of the cargo against which the drafts were drawn in any case?

A. No, sir.

77 Q. Had A. F. Smith & Co. received cargoes by vessels against which drafts were drawn on them which came forward through the Merchants' Bank of Watertown and the City Bank of Oswego before the receipt of the eight cargoes in question in these cases?

A. Yes, sir; frequently during the years 1868 and 1869.

Q. What is the date of the failure of A. F. Smith & Co.?

A. I think it was the 15th or 16th of October last; it was not earlier than the 15th.

Q. Before the date of your failure, did the Merchants' Bank at Watertown or the City Bank of Oswego, or any of their officers, look after or make any inquiries respecting the disposition of any wheat received from any of these vessels, at the time of its receipt at the Corn Exchange elevator or at any time afterward?

A. No, sir; not to my knowledge.

Q. Did Mr. Mannering, cashier of the City Bank, call upon you for insurance at or about the time of the receipt of the cargo of the Atwater or the Fort?

78 A. He did call for some insurance, but don't recollect the date; he did call about that time.

Q. Did you give him a certificate of insurance for the amount he called for?

A. I think I did or directed it to be given to him.

Q. Did you afterwards receive from the City Bank the certificates that had been given the bank?

A. Yes, sir; I have looked for these certificates and could find none that I could identify as held by the bank.

Q. In whose name was the insurance in those certificates effected?

A. In the name of A. F. Smith & Co.

Q. How was the property insured in these certificates described?

A. I think it was described substantially as on Exhibit C (A. B. G.) annexed to the deposition of David Mannering, and is described " as grain, their own or held by them on commission, or sold but not delivered, contained in the Corn Exchange elevator."

Q. Did the bank also hold policies of insurance effected by you?

A. It did.

79 Q. How was the property insured described in those policies?

A. Substantially as in the policy marked Exhibit D (A. B. G.), annexed to the deposition of David Mannering.

Q. How is the property described in that policy, Exhibit D?

A. As grain, flour, and other produce, their own or held by them on commission or sold and not delivered, contained in the Corn Exchange elevator.

Q. Did A. F. Smith & Co. have or effect insurance in any other form?

A. No, sir; not on contents in the elevator.

Q. Did they ever effect insurance on any wheat or grain in the elevator held simply on storage as warehousemen?

A. No, sir.

Q. Were the certificates given to Mr. Mannering upon any particular lot or cargo of grain?

A. No, sir.

Q. What was the object of policy in the hands of Mr. Mannering or the City Bank certificates of insurance or policies of insurance?

80   A. I suppose they were to be held by the bank as a sort of collateral security for the payment of any acceptance they might hold of ours, in case of a loss by fire disabling us from meeting our engagements.

Q. On receipt of the several cargoes of the eight vessels, did A. F. Smith & Co. sell or dispose of it by shipments to New York, under advances, without reference to the maturity of the time drafts?

A. Yes, sir.

Q. Did either the Merchants' Bank at Watertown or the City Bank of Oswego ever give you any express authority, before or after the maturity of the time drafts, to sell or dispose of any of these cargoes?

A. No, sir; we made none, and never asked for any.

Q. Did you, or the firm of A. F. Smith & Co., receive from the City Bank of Oswego any order, request, or direction to ship any of the cargoes of either the Atwater or the Fort?

A. No, sir.

Q. Were the said shipments of the said cargoes made, as far as you know, without the knowledge or consent of the City Bank of Oswego?

A. Yes, sir.

81   Q. When, as far as you know, did the City Bank of Oswego first know or learn of the shipments of the cargoes of the Atwater and Fort?

A. Shortly after our suspension, I suppose, they first learned it.

Q. Had the firm of A. F. Smith & Co. received any, and how many, cargoes of wheat from Mower, Church & Bell, of Milwaukee, prior to the order for the cargoes of the Atwater and D. G. Fort, which had been ordered partly on sight drafts and partly on time drafts, and which cargoes had been consigned for the account of Milwaukee banks in care of banks at Oswego?

A. We had purchased some grain from Mower, Church & Bell prior to the cargoes of the Atwater and Fort; how many cargoes I don't recollect; I don't recollect how they were consigned, but presume they were consigned in the same way as the cargoes of the Atwater and Fort.

Q. Have you any doubt that the consignments were the same?

A. I think they were the same.

Q. How many, or about how many, cargoes were there consigned prior to the cargoes of the Atwater and Fort?

A. I should think two or three, at least.

82   Q. In each of the said cases, was the sight-draft paid and the time-draft accepted prior to the cargo reaching Oswego?

A. Yes, sir; I think so.

Q. Did not the firm of A. F. Smith & Co. know the exact character of said former shipments from Mower, Church & Bell at or before payment of the sight-drafts and acceptance of the time-drafts attached to the bills of lading of the cargoes of the Atwater and D. G. Fort?

A. We did know the manner the business was done, so far as we were concerned.

Q. Did not said firm of A. F. Smith & Co. know that bills of lading were always given at Milwaukee to the bank or banks at Milwaukee, on discount by said bank or banks of the drafts drawn by said Mower, Church & Bell on said A. F. Smith & Co.?

A. I have no means of knowing where the bank obtained the bill of lading.

Q. Did the drafts, sight and time, always come to Oswego attached to the bill of lading of the cargo in cases when the property was, by the bill of lading, for the account of the Milwaukee bank, or its cashier, in the care of an Oswego bank?

83   A. I don't know, when they came to Oswego, whether they were or not; they were usually attached when presented to us for payment and acceptance.

Q. Where there were time drafts on the cargoes were the bills of lading ever surrendered by the bank at Oswego, in whose care the cargo was consigned, until payment of the time drafts?

A. I think they were usually held in the custody of the bank, and were not surrendered to us. I mean by "us," A. F. Smith & Co.

Q. Under the circumstances mentioned in the last preceding interrogatory, did A. F. Smith & Co. ever receive, directly from Milwaukee, a bill of lading of a cargo?

A. No, sir.

Q. Did the bill of lading, under such circumstances, always go to the bank at Oswego, as far as you know?

A. Yes, sir.

Q. Did not A. F. Smith & Co. know that the Oswego banks, in cases of time drafts drawn on cargoes, were instructed by the Milwaukee

84   banks for whose account the cargo, by the bills of lading, were shipped, to hold the said cargoes, and for said banks, until payment of the time drafts?

A. No, sir.

Q. Look upon the letter now show you, purporting to be a letter from A. F. Smith & Co., dated Sept. 14, 1869, addressed to Messrs. Mower, Church & Bell, and state in whose hand is the said letter, and in whose handwriting is the signature on the said letter.

A. It is in my handwriting.

Q. Was it written at or about its date?

A. I have no doubt it was.

Q. What do the words in the said letter " We cannot but think that your bank is over-particular in its instructions to its correspondent here; more so, in fact, than any other in your city with which we have had dealings " refer to or mean?

A. It refers to the instructions given to the City Bank of Oswego, of which the cashier informed us in relation to this particular instance. That letter assumes that other banks had not given as stringent instructions, because we had never been advised or heard of similar in-

85   structions from other banks.

Q. Did the firm of A. F. Smith & Co. receive from Mower, Church & Bell, or either of them, a reply to the said letter?

A. I think we received a reply to it.

Q. So far as you know, were the consignments in the case of the Atwater and the D. G. Fort any different from the prior cargoes shipped by Mower, Church & Bell to Oswego?

A. I conclude the instructions were different, as the matters which we had previously objected to were not insisted upon in those cases.

Q. What were the matters which you had previously objected to, which were not insisted upon in the case of the Atwater and the D. G. Fort; please specify.

A. In giving a warehouse receipt for the property.

Q. Is that all?

A. I think of nothing else to which we objected.

Q. Did you, in each of the other instances, know of instruction being given to take warehouse receipts?

A. Mr. Mannering told me, in one instance, that their instruc-

86   tions required them to take warehouse receipts, but only in one instance.

Q. When did Mannering tell you that, and in relation to what cargo?

A. I cannot tell; don't recollect the time or the occasion. I presume it was about the date of that letter.

Q. What makes you presume it was about the date of that letter?

A. Because that letter referred to instructions given by the Milwaukee bank to our correspondent, and it is very natural I should write, after that conversation, to Mower, Church & Bell.

Q. Did the firm of A. F. Smith & Company ever write any other letter than the one shown you, in relation to instructions given by the Milwaukee bank to its correspondent in Oswego?

A. I don't recollect.

Q. Did not the firm of A. F. Smith & Co. write a letter dated Sept. 1st, 1869, addressed to Mower, Church & Bell, on the subject of the Milwaukee bank instructions to its correspondent in Oswego, in which they used this language, "But your bank say, in their instructions, to hold the property, and as soon as a certain draft is paid, they
87   may deliver grain enough to amount to that," or words to that effect?

A. I find upon our books a copy of a letter of that date in which words to that effect are used.

Q. Were the said drafts attached to bills of lading of the cargoes of the Atwater and the D. G. Fort at the time the same were accepted by A. F. Smith & Co.?

A. I presume they were.

Q. Have you any doubt that they were?

A. I have no doubt they were attached when they were presented to us; that was the usual manner in which they came to us.

Q. When the captains arrived with cargoes at Oswego consigned for the account of the Milwaukee banks in care of the Oswego banks or the Merchants' Bank, did they or not, in the usual course of business, exhibit to the warehousemen or receive from warehousemen their orders to deliver the cargoes?

A. I suppose they received their orders from the consignees. I suppose that was where the captains got their orders.

Q. Was that the usual course of business at Oswego?

A. So far as I know it was.

88   Q. When the order was sent to the warehouse, as in the case of the Merchants' Bank, did the captains call for and receive their orders for the delivery of the cargoes?

A. I suppose they would call wherever they supposed the order to be.

Q. In the cases of the shipments made by Mower, Church & Bell, by bills of lading for account of the Milwaukee banks in the care of the City Bank of Oswego, were the orders of delivery usually endorsed or written on the captains' bills of lading?

A. As far as I know, that was the custom of the City Bank.

Q. Did Mr. Forsyth sign the receipt for a large portion of the wheat or grain which went into the Corn Exchange elevator, or consignments from Milwaukee for the account of the Milwaukee banks in care of the City Bank of Oswego, or the Merchants' Bank in the name of A. F. Smith & Co.?

A. Mr. Forsyth usually settled with the captains, and signed the receipts for the cargoes and statements of freight paid.

Q. Had he authority to sign receipts for A. F. Smith & Co. on the captains' bills of lading?

89   A. Yes, sir.

Q. What did you mean when, in answer to the question put to you by the defendant's counsel, as to whether A. F. Smith & Co. were advised of any special directions or instructions accompanying bills of lading sent to the City Bank of Oswego, you stated not to your knowledge?

A. I meant that neither our Milwaukee correspondent nor the Milwaukee banks had advised us of any special instructions, nor had the City Bank in these instances.

Q. Is that all you meant by that answer to this question?

A. Yes, sir; that is all I meant.

Q. Is it true that A. F. Smith & Co. could not have been advised of the special directions or instructions accompanying the bills of lading sent to the City Bank of Oswego or to the Merchants' Bank after the receipt by them of the letters or orders for the delivery of the cargoes?

A. I don't know that it is true that they could not have been advised, but it is true that they were not so advised, so far as I know.

Q. Did you not, as one of the firm of A. F. Smith & Co., know 90   by the terms of the letters and orders sent by the Merchants' Bank and by the orders endorsed on the captain's bill of lading that the grain was to be delivered to A. F. Smith & Co., or the Corn Exchange elevator, for the account of the cashiers of the different plaintiffs in these suits, subject to the orders of the banks, until the payment of the drafts mentioned in said letters or orders.

A. No, sir; I don't know that I did.

MAY 11, 1870.

Q. Please explain what you mean by your last answer?

A. I don't know what explanation it needs.

Q. Do you mean that the said letters or orders were not explicit in their terms; that the cargoes referred to were not to be delivered to A. F. Smith & Co. until the payment of the drafts therein mentioned?

A. The letters from the Merchants' Bank were explicit, expressed their instruction what they desired; but I did not understand from them that we were not to have the wheat, because the wheat came into our possession without any difficulty. We understood when we bought the wheat we were to have it, and we got it.

91   Q. Was it for that reason and no other that A. F. Smith & Co. shipped, or caused to be shipped, said wheat, and all of it?

A. We sold it because we considered it our own, and disposed of it as our own.

Q. In cases where grain was delivered to the Corn Exchange elevator from lake vessels, which by the bill of lading purported to be for Milwaukee banks, in care of Oswego banks, was it or not in the usual course of business, the custom of A. F. Smith & Co. to to advance or pay the lake freights on delivery into said warehouse?

A. When the property was ours, and not in other cases.

Q. When grain was delivered into the Corn Exchange elevator, an order, such as you have testified to, were usually given by the City Bank of Oswego in cases of cargoes consigned for account of Milwaukee banks in care of said City Bank of Oswego, who, according to the usual course of business, paid or advanced the lake freights?

A. Most of the cargoes consigned in that way were our own, and the freights were paid by us in these cases.

92   Q. Were you present when the cashier of the City Bank of Oswego gave in his testimony, or did you hear read his testimony?

A. I was present when a portion of his testimony was given.

Q. Did you hear that portion of his testimony relating to the asking for insurance on the cargoes of the Atwater and the Fort?

A. I don't think I heard that portion of his testimony.

Q. Did the cashier of the City Bank of Oswego ask A. F. Smith & Co. for insurance on said cargoes, or either of them?

A. He asked for some more insurance than that already held by the bank, not having quite enough to cover the drafts against the cargoes of the Atwater & Fort.

Q. Did A. F. Smith & Co. give or pretend to give the insurance he asked for.

A. We directed an additional certificate of insurance to be given.

Q. Did they endorse said certificate of insurance?

A. I think they did not on this occasion.

Q. Do you know that they did not?

93   A. My recollection is that Mr. Mannering and Mr. Newkirk, an insurance agent, were at our office together, and to save time, I requested Mr. Newkirk to give Mr. Mannering a certificate for what he required.

Q. And did he do so?

A. I suppose he did.

Q. You stated on your cross-examination, did you not, in substance, that as to the cargoes which came into your possession through the banks, under acceptances drawn against them, prior to the receipt of the wheat by the eight vessels, you sold, or disposed of said cargoes without reference to the maturity of the time drafts, at any time after the payment of the sight drafts and acceptance of the time drafts; were said shipments or sales, as far as you know, made with the knowledge or consent of the banks, in whose care the cargoes were consigned.

A. I think I so stated.   We had no express consent, and I don't know that they had any knowledge of shipments or sales.

Q. Was there any understanding, arrangement, or agreement, between A. F. Smith & Co., and the City Bank of Oswego, or the Mer-

94   chants' Bank, at Watertown, that A. F. Smith & Co. might, or could, sell or dispose of the sight cargoes in question, or any or either of them until payment of the several drafts drawn on the several cargoes?

A. There was not to my knowledge.

Q. Was it or not in accordance with the usual and ordinary course of business at the Corn Exchange Elevator in case of the receipt of grain from lake vessels, simply for storage or transshipment, for the proprietors of said elevator to advance or pay the freight on cargoes thus received?

A. Not unless the cargoes were owned by or consigned to A. F. Smith & Co.   When grain was simply stored for other parties, we never paid freights.

Q. Did you see the order testified too by Mr. Mannering, as written by him on the face of the captain's bill of lading of the Atwater and the Fort?

A. I don't recollect whether I saw it or not.

Q. Will you look at these orders testified to by him, and now shown you, or the copies thereof now shown you, on Exhibits Nos. 16 and 18,

95   attached to the deposition of Mannering, and state if that was the usual form of orders given by the City Bank to captains of

vessels with cargoes, consigned by bill of lading to the City Bank, holding drafts against the cargoes on A. F. Smith & Co. ?

A. I think it was the usual form.

Q. Did A. F. Smith & Co. receive from the City Bank any order or direction as to the disposition of either the wheat by the Atwater or the Fort, before, on, or after the receipt of the wheat at the Corn Exchange Elevator?

A. None to my knowledge.

Q. Was there any express agreement in respect to the payment of the freight on wheat, by either the Atwater or Fort, between the City Bank, of Oswego, and A. F. Smith & Co. ?

A. No, sir.

Q. Is it not the general usage where cargoes are delivered to the party upon whom drafts against it are drawn, for such parties to pay the freight?

A. It is.

Q. Did the City Bank make any arrangement or provision for the payment of the freight by A. F. Smith & Co. on the wheat by either
96   the Atwater or the Fort, except by delivery of the wheat by those vessels to A. F. Smith & Co., or at their elevator?

A. No, sir.

Q. According to the course of business at the Corn Exchange Elevator, where property is received merely on storage, as warehouse men for other parties, do A. F. Smith & Co. pay either freight or insurance?

A. No, sir.

Q. Will you look at the paper now shown you, of which a copy is annexed and marked Exhibit W. N., No. 1, (A. B. G.), and state whether you are able to identify that as the certificate of insurance given by A. F. Smith & Co., or by their direction to Mr. Mannering?

A. I think this is the same one.

Q. Do you recollect the circumstances under which that was given?

A. I think I do. I think Mr. Mannering came over to the office and asked for some additional insurance. Mr. Newkirk, insurance agent, being also present, I requested him to give Mr. Mannering a certificate
97   for the amount he required, which I think was five thousand dollars. I think I asked him to make the loss, if any, payable to the City Bank. That was to avoid the necessity of accompanying Mr. Newkirk to his office and then endorsing the certificate.

Q. What was the date of the delivery of that certificate of insurance to Mr. Mannering—on or about what date?

A. On or about the 9th of October, 1869.

Q. Is there any writing on that certificate in the handwriting of Mr. Mannering, the cashier of the City Bank?

A. I think the words "for 15 days from date" are in the handwriting of Mr. Mannering.

Q. Will you explain how this certificate of insurance, dated on the 4th of Oct., was given out the ninth?

A. I can't explain why it was given on the ninth any more fully than I have done, but can explain why it was dated on the 4th. I suppose it was because the insurance was procured on the 4th.

Q. Had the firm of A. F. Smith & Co. a standing policy with Mr. Newkirk?

A. Yes, sir; and, having shipped out property between the
98   4th and 9th of Oct., I desired Mr. Newkirk to transfer five thousand dollars of insurance with him to the City Bank, of Oswego,

and he made that transfer on the 9th by the delivery of the papers to Mr. Mannering, I suppose.

Redirect:

Q. (By Mr. FINCH.) What was the market value of No. 1 Milwaukee wheat at Oswego at or during the period of time from Sept. 16, 1869, to Oct. 14th, 1869?

A. The market value of such wheat was as follows, on the following days:

Sept. 16, 1869		$1. 47½ per bushel.
" 20, "		1. 42 " "
" 24, "	1. 39 & 1. 40	" "
" 27, "		1. 40 " "
" 28, "		1. 38 " "
" 30, "		1. 38 " "
Oct. 1st, "		1. 35 " "
" 5th, "	1. 30 @ 1. 34	" "
" 9th, "		1. 30 " "
" 11, "		1. 25 " "
" 14,	1. 28 @ 1. 29	" "

Q. What was the market value of No. 2 Milwaukee wheat at 99   Oswego at and during the period of time from Sept., 1869, to October 14, 1869?

A. The market value of such wheat was as follows on the following days:

Sept. 20		$1.35 per bushel.
" 22		1.32 " "
" 29		1.30 " "
Oct. 11		1.17 " "

Q. Are the amounts made from actual rates of wheat on the days mentioned?

A. They are.

Forty-fourth. A. F. Smith & Co. shipped out of the elevator of the cargo of the Atwater into the canal boat E. N. Shepard, on the 9th day of October, 7,641.26 bushels of wheat, and consigned the same to John Wilmot; that A. F. Smith & Co. drew a draft upon said shipment on John Wilmot, of New York, for $8,415.10, and attached the same to a bill of lading given by the captain of said canal boat; that John Wilmot paid the draft; that plaintiff brought suit against said Wilmot for said wheat and recovered a judgment therein.

Forty-fifth. That A. F. Smith & Co. shipped out of the elevator of the cargo of the D. G. Fort, into the canal boat Moses Melvin, 7,650 bushels of wheat and received from the captain of said canal boat a bill of lading therefor consigning the same to said Wilmot; that said 100   shipment was made October 9th, 1869; that A. F. Smith & Co. drew a draft upon said John Wilmot for $8,415; that said Wilmot paid said draft and received said wheat; that plaintiff brought suit in the United States court in and for the southern district of New York to recover the full value of said wheat, and recovered a judgment therein.

Forty-sixth. That the said defendant is incorporated under the laws of the State of New York as alleged in the answer.

Forty-seventh. On the 12th day of November, 1869, a notice was served on the defendant, the City Bank, of which the following is a copy:

REC. 473--3

To the City Bank of Oswego, Oswego, N. Y.:

Please take notice that the Milwaukee National Bank of Wisconsin has this day commenced a suit in the circuit court of the United States in and for the eastern district of New York against the firm of Hughes, Hickcox & Co., of New York City, and also John Wilmot, of the same place, to recover the value of certain wheat which was shipped from Milwaukee, Wisconsin, in the schooner Atwater and D. G.
101   Fort, consigned to ⅗ of T. L. Baker, cashier, in care of City Bank, Oswego, and as we are informed by your bank directed to be delivered into the " Corn Exchange Elevator," at Oswego, and which said wheat was afterwards (as it is said) shipped out of said elevator by the proprietors thereof and sent in canal boats to the said Hughes, Hickcox & Co. and John Wilmot, and you are hereby notified that the said Milwaukee National Bank of Wisconsin looks to you to furnish it with such competent and legal evidence as may be in your power, or under your control, or which you can obtain, going to show that the title of the said wheat was not lost or impaired by any act or omission of yours or any persons connected with you, and to procure said evidence we will cheerfully and heartily co operate with you in any and all proper and legal measures to obtain said evidence, and you are at liberty to and may communicate and confer with our attorneys, Messrs. Porter, Lowery & Loven, of 78 Broadway, New York City, and we further notify you that in case of any judgment or verdict adverse to our title to the said wheat, or any part thereof, by reason of any ne-
102   glect, failure, default, or act of yours, your agents, servants, officers, or employees, or any of them, that we shall hold you responsible for the full value of the said wheat, and for all costs, charges, expenses and disbursements, with interest, incurred in or about the said suits or to obtain the said wheat or its value with interest therein. These suits are brought by us on the representations of the cashier and officers of your bank that nothing has been done or omitted by the bank, its officers or agents to impair or destroy our title, and with no desire or intent on our part to waive our claim against you or in any way to impair the same.

And we further notify you that there is now pending in the supreme court of the State of New York, in and for the county of Oswego, a suit against A. F. Smith and Sidney Bickford, for a conversion of the said wheat above mentioned, and that we shall look to you for indemnity for all costs, charges, expenses and disbursements in the said suit, and for the value of the wheat so converted or taken by said A. F. Smith & Co., and that you may (if you can) show that the said A. F. Smith &
103   Co. had no lawful or rightful claim to said wheat or any part thereof, and that you did not omit to take all needful and proper acts to keep the said wheat for said Milwaukee National Bank of Wisconsin, and that you did no act to give said Smith & Co., or either member of the said firm, any lawful or rightful authority or control over the said wheat or any part thereof. We hereby request you to communicate with our attorneys in said suit, G. G. French, esq., of Mexico, N. Y., and give him all necessary and rightful aid and assistance.

THE MERCHANTS' NATIONAL BANK OF WISCONSIN,
By E. CRAMER, *President.*
T. L. BAKER, *Cashier.*

Forty-eighth. In the month of December, 1869, a notice was served on the defendant, of which the following is a copy:

To the City Bank of Oswego, and Delos DeWolf its president, and David Mannering its cashier:

We have received a notice this day from you, dated December 4th, 1869, stating that two suits have been instituted against the City Bank of Oswego, in the supreme court of the State of New York, one by Samuel V. Parsons and John Hamble, as owners of the schooner D. G. Fort, claiming to recover $1,201.56, and interest thereon; and the other in favor of John T. Davison, Hosea Rogers, and George Hardison, as owners of the schooner Atwater, claiming to recover $1,511.43, with interest, &c. The cargoes of wheat mentioned in the said notice were consigned "to the account or order of T. L. Baker, cashier, in the care of the City Bank of Oswego." Letters were written by said Baker to you, or some one of you, expressly notifying you that the firm of A. F. Smith & Co. were to pay the freight on these cargoes, and instructing you that on payment of the freight and certain drafts you might deliver the said cargoes of wheat. You had, therefore, no legal right to deliver the wheat to A. F. Smith & Co., or any other parties, except upon the condition that the freight was paid. We are informed (but whether or not such is the fact you know and we do not) that in violation of these instructions you gave an order to the captains of the lake vessels in these words, "Deliver the within cargo of wheat to the Corn Exchange Elevator for and on account of T. L. Baker, cashier, subject to the order of the City Bank of Oswego," without specifying anything in relation to the payment of freight, and not in any way or by any act except by said order retaining possession or custody or control of said wheat for the payment of the freight.

And we are further informed that at the time you so gave such order you well knew that A. F. Smith & Co. were the sole lessees or proprietors of the Corn Exchange Elevator, and well knew that the wheat was delivered in pursuance of your order. We, therefore, claim that by so doing you violated our instructions, and that you are liable to respond to us for any and all sums of money which we may be liable to pay by reason or account of your disregard of our instructions. Without waiving or being understood as in any manner waiving any of our rights against you or either of you, and without in any way admitting that you have any right to call upon us to take any part in the suits mentioned in your notice, but on the contrary asserting and claiming that as against you we have a right to ask, sue for, receive, or recover every cent of money in your hands which was paid to you for our account, and protesting that you have no claim upon us, and no right to call upon us to take notice of the suits mentioned by you, we hereby notify you that subject to each and all of these conditions, reservations, and protestations, we will name George G. French, esq., of Mexico, Oswego County, New York, our attorney, to represent us in said suits, so far as may be necessary to show that the funds now belonging to us in your hands ought not to be detained by you by reason or on account of the said suits mentioned in your notices or either of them, and that the owners of the said vessels and each of them have received payment of their freight; and we further notify you that we shall, notwithstanding the said suits, and your notice of them, hold you responsible for the said money in your hands belonging to us, and interest thereon from the day you received the same, and also shall look to

107   you to pay and reimburse us for any and all sums of money paid or disbursed by us in or about the recovery of said money.
Dated Milwaukee, Dec. 10th, 1869.
THE MILWAUKEE NATIONAL BANK OF WISCONSIN,
By GEORGE G. FRENCH, *Its Attorney.*

Forty-ninth. On the 21st day of May, 1870, a notice was served on the defendant, of which the following is a copy:

Circuit court of the United States in and for the southern district *district* of New York.

THE MILWAUKEE NATIONAL BANK OF WIS-
        consin, plaintiff,
            against
ARTHUR HUGHES, CHARLES R. HICKCOX, AND
    John M. Hughes, def'ts.

THE MILWAUKEE NATIONAL BANK OF WIS-
        consin, plaintiff,
            against
JOHN WILMOT, DEFENDANT.

To the City Bank of Oswego:

Please take notice that the above-entitled causes and each of them are now pending in the said above-entitled court; that the said causes and each of them are actions of trover to recover damages for the
108   conversion by the defendants of a quantity of wheat, portions of the cargoes of the schooners Atwater and D. G. Fort, and which said cargoes were consigned by the said plaintiff to the care of the City Bank of Oswego, and the bills of lading of the said cargoes, with certain drafts drawn on A. F. Smith & Co., were transmitted by the said plaintiff to the said the City Bank of Oswego, with instruction that on payment of the said drafts the said wheat was to be delivered to A. F. Smith & Co.

And you will further take notice that the said defendants and each of them have appeared in the said respective suits in which they are named as parties defendants, and have filed in the said cause the plea of the general issue, and that under the said plea of the general issue it is absolutely essential to the plaintiff's right to recover in the said suits to show its title to the said wheat, and that the defendants and each of them have unlawfully or wrongfully obtained the said wheat or that portion of it which it is claimed they wrongfully and unlawfully converted of the cargoes of the schooner Atwater and D. G. Fort.

109   And you will further take notice that the said defendants and each of them give out, pretend, and claim that they have a good, valid, and lawful title to the said wheat or that portion thereof in their hands of the wheat of the said cargoes Atwater and D. G. Fort, by purchase or otherwise, from A. F. Smith & Co., or parties claiming title under said firm of A. F. Smith & Co., and that the said plaintiff as against them has no lawful right or claim to the said wheat or any portion thereof.

And you further take notice that if the said pretence or claim of the said defendants or either of them is sustained, then the said plaintiff in each of the said suits will lose its title to the said wheat involved in the said suits without the payment of the drafts or some of them on said

A. F. Smith & Co., and by the act of the City Bank of Oswego in delivering the said wheat to A. F. Smith & Co. without payment thereof, and in direct violation of the instructions given by said plaintiff to the said bank, or in not taking sufficient, or proper, or legal steps to keep, maintain, and hold the identical wheat of said cargoes for said plaintiff until said drafts were paid.

110

And you will further take notice that you are herewith required and requested to take the prosecution of the above-entitled causes and each of them into your own hands (and the same is hereby tendered and offered to you), and you are hereby further required to assert, as far as you can, by all lawful and proper means the title of the said plaintiff to the wheat in question in the said two causes and each of them, and to hold the said plaintiff harmless from all costs, charges, and expenses of every name, nature, character, and description whatsoever in and about the prosecution of the said suits or either of them.

And you will further take notice that in case of your refusal to take upon yourself the prosecution of the said suits and each of them, then the said plaintiff, hereby requests you to furnish the said plaintiff, if you can, with proper and legal evidence to enable the plaintiff to trace out the identical wheat of the said cargoes of the schooners Atwater and D. G. Fort, and to hold the title thereto as against the said defendants or either of them.

111

And you will further take notice that the said plaintiff, in case of your neglect or failure or refusal to take upon yourself the prosecution of the said suits, or either of them, will hold you responsible, and will look to you for full indemnity for all costs, charges, disbursements, and expenses made by it in and about the prosecution of the said suits and each of them, and in case of defeat therein, and loss of the title of the wheat involved in said causes, or either of them, for the full value thereof and interest thereon.

And in case of your neglect or refusal to give or furnish legal and competent evidence to enable the plaintiff to trace out the identical wheat of the said cargoes, and so as to enable the plaintiff to hold the title thereto as against the said defendants, or either of them, it will hold you responsible for the full value of the said wheat involved in the said suits, or either of them, with interest, and for all costs, charges, expenses, and disbursements and interest thereon in and about the said suits.

112

Yours, &c.,

THE MILWAUKEE NATIONAL BANK OF WISCONSIN,

By H. M. FINCH,

Its Att'y.

MAY 19*th*, 1870.

Fiftieth. In January, 1873, a notice of which the following is a copy was served on the defendant, to wit:

MILWAUKEE, *January 24th*, 1873.

To the City Bank of Oswego, Delos De Wolf, and David Mannering:

GENTLEMEN: Herewith find a printed case, which we propose to stipulate to be used in the case of the Milwaukee National Bank of Wisconsin vs. Arthur Hughes, Charles R. Hickcox, and John M. Hughes. We desire your especial attention to the same. If there are any additions, alterations, or suggestions which you desire made, let us know without delay. We want you to be fully posted of our doings, as, if this case goes against the plaintiff, we shall look to you for the

113   value of the wheat in said suit, and all costs, charges, and expenses incurred in   about the same. We do not know the precise day when this cause will be called for trial. If you desire any other or different testimony, or other or different facts to go into the case, please let us know at an early day. We will delay sending the cases forward to the defendants for a few days in order to hear from you.

.Respectfully yours, &c.,

H. M. FINCH,
Att'y for the Milwaukee National Bank of Wisconsin.

Fifty-first. On the eighteenth day of February, 1874, a notice was served on the defendant, of which the following is a copy, to wit:

Supreme court.

JOHN T. DAVISON, HOSEA ROGERS, AND GEORGE
Hardison, respondents,
against
THE CITY BANK, APPELLANT.

SAMUEL V. PARSONS AND JOHN HUMBLE, RE-
spondents,
ag'st
THE CITY BANK, APPELLANT.

114   To the City Bank, Oswego:

You will take notice that the Milwaukee National Bank of Wisconsin, by George G. French, its attorney, has paid to the plaintiffs in the first above entitled action, the sum of two thousand four hundred and thirty-eight and $\frac{40}{100}$ dollars, and have paid to the plaintiffs in the second above entitled action the sum of two thousand thirty-nine and $\frac{37}{100}$ dollars on account of the claims described in complaints herein respectively; protesting, nevertheless, that the necessity for such payment has arisen from the omissions and neglect of duty by you, the said The City Bank, your officers and agents, in violation of the instructions to you from the said Milwaukee National Bank of Wisconsin, its officers and agents, as described in the notice from the said Milwaukee National Bank of Wisconsin to you, the said The City Bank of Oswego, dated on or about December 10th, 1869, and served on you on or about December 16th, 1869; and from the other circumstances described in such notice you will also take notice that

115 ,116   the Milwaukee National Bank of Wisconsin will hold you responsible, and will require, and hereby requests you to pay the said amounts and the expenses incurred in the defense of the above entitled actions and the value of the said wheat cargoes of the said schooners D. G. Fort and Atwater, described in said notice so heretofore served upon you.

Dated February 16th, 1874.

MILWAUKEE NATIONAL BANK OF WISCONSIN,
By GEO. G. FRENCH,
Its Att'y.

1869.					1869.				
Aug.	2	To check		125 06	Aug.	1	By balance		317 67
"	4	" "		6,000	"	3	" checks		7,136 24
"	7	" "		540 36	"	7	" "		15,052 24
"	"	" "		7,000	"	12	" "		2,072 32
"	11	" " 8,900, 414.30		9,314 30	"	13	" "		13,438 80
"	13	" " 5,000, 987.20		5,987 20	"	17	" "		12,977 84
"	14	" " 340.25, 14		354 25	"	19	" "		200
"	17	" "		2,120	"	21	" A. F. Smith & Co. on Smith, Wemple & Co. 20 days from date due Sept. 13th,	$5,000	
"	19	" " 6,000, 5,000		11,000			Less dis't	47 05	4,052 95
"	"	" "		1,490 32	"	24	" check		191 50
"	20	" "		126	"	"	" Smith, Wemple & Co. on John Taylor's Sons, 60 days from date, due Oct. 16th	$10,250	
"	21	" stamp		2 50			Less dis't	189 59	10,060 41
"	23	" check, 1,529.52, 5,000		6,529 52	"	26	" checks		10,989
"	24	" "		5,000	"	31	" "		2,329 60
"	26	" "		8,900	Sep.	1	" A. F. Smith & Co. on Franklin, Edson & Co., 15 days from date, due Sept. 19th	10,495 80	
"	"	" " 1,016, 495.97		1,511 97			Less disc't	88 71	10,407 09
"	27	" "		5,000	"	2	" checks		4,959 87
"	30	" "		570 60	"	"	" "		278 74
"	31	" "		2,000	"	"	" A. F. Smith & Co. on Smith, Wemple & Co., 15 days from date, due Sept. 20th	7,000	
Sep.	1	" stamps		5 30			Less disc't	59 16	6,940 84
"	"	" check		2,000	"	4	" checks		5,444 11
"	2	" stamps		3 50	"	"	" A. F. Smith & Co. on Franklin, Edson & Co., 15 days from date, due Sept. 22d	5,449 56	
"	"	" check		6,000			Less disc't	46 06	5,403 50
"	"	" " 66, 6,487.48		6,553 48	"	4	" A. F. Smith & Co. on Franklin, Edson & Co., 20 days from date, due Sep. 27	5,449 56	
"	"	" " 23.01, 485		508 01			Less disc't	51 29	5,398 27
"	3	" "		327	"	4	" A. F. Smith on Franklin, Edson & Co., 25 days from date, due Oct. 2d	5,549 56	
"	4	" stamps		8 25			Less disc't	56 51	5,393 05
"	"	" check, 21,798.24, 2,403		24,201 24	"	7	" checks		7,258
"	"	" " 5,000, 42.81		5,042 81	"	11	" "		607 96
"	7	" " 5,000, 2,503.25		7,503 25	"	17	" "		11,905 08
"	10	" "		50 80	"	21	" "		431 92
"	11	" "		55 50					
"	13	" " 300, 400		700					
"	16	" " 370.19, 400		770 19					
"	17	" "		10,000					
"	18	" "		1,083 24					
"	20	" "		400					
"	22	" "		565 74					
"	23	" stamps		2 50					
"	"	" check		5,000					
Oct.	4	" " 4,052.62, 1,000.80		5,053 42					
"	9	" " 9,500, 2,000		11,500					
"	12	" int. on F. & R. check		7 29					

Dr.

Date		Particulars	Amount	
	13	To check	60	
	14	" " 203.80, 84, 250, 54.76	592	56
	"	" " 9,500, 300	9,800	00
	15	" " 87.04, 332.18	419	22
	16	" error in rebate	47	56
	25	" prot. 4th Nat	20	04
		Balance	1	56
			163	32
118				
			178,226	45
1870.				
Jan.	18	To check, 428, 211.18	639	18
	20	" "	29	23
Feb.	7	" "	25	
	10	" "	100	
	16	" "	424	
	18	" "	30	
	"	" "	374	48
	21	" "	6	
	24	" "	25	
	26	" "	95	
Mar.	1	" " 35.30	65	
	2	" "	30	
	3	" "	11	
	4	" "	20	
	7	" "	44	09
	8	" " 25, 18.79, 3	48	79
	9	" "	9	50
	"	" "	55	86
	10	" "	50	
	12	" "	50	
	14	" "	40	75
	23	" "	404	
April	5	" "	56	40
May	30	" int. on overdraft	4	02
			2,631	30

Cr.

Date		Particulars		Amount	
	23	By A. F. Smith & Co. on Smith, Wemple & Co., 15 days from date, due Oct. 11th	5,000		
		Less disc't	42 26		
				4,957	74
	30	" checks		550	
Oct.	4	" "		5,100	
	9	" "		12,675	
	14	" "		9,876	67
	"	" rebate, wrong entry		20	04
				178,226	45
		Balance forward			
1869.					
		By balance forward		163	32
1870.					
Jan.	18	" cash		886	
Feb.	15	" "		431	17
	16	" "		400	
	24	" "		185	
Mar.	10	" "		412	
	22	" "		100	
	30	" " of A. F. Smith		53	81
				2,631	30

119   Circuit court of the United States for the northern district of
New York.

THE MILWAUKEE NATIONAL BANK OF WISCON-
sin
vs.
THE CITY BANK.

It is hereby stipulated by and between the attorneys for the respective parties to this action that upon the trial thereof either party may read as testimony as follows:

First. The whole or any part of the printed case made up in the suit of The Milwaukee National Bank of Wisconsin against Arthur Hughes, Charles R. Hickcox and John M. Hughes, and hereto annexed, as corrected, except the portions thereof which have been erased.

Second. The whole or any part of the annexed matter in manuscript from and including the article thereof numbered "thirty-ninth" to and including the article numbered "fifty-first."

Third. The whole or any part of the depositions of A. F. Smith
120   and Sidney Bickford, taken at Oswego, by and before Alfred B. Getty, U. S. commissioner, on the 2d, 3rd, and 4th days of October, 1872, in three suits pending in the circuit court of the United States for the southern district of New York, against John Wilmot, and printed.

Fourth. The whole or any part of the depositions of Ananias F. Smith and Sidney Bickford, taken at Mexico, in the County of Oswego, N. Y., on the 17th day of February, 1870, by and before Cyrus Whitney, esquire, Oswego County judge, in an action pending in the supreme court of the State of New York, between the Milwaukee National Bank of Wisconsin, as plaintiff, and said Ananias F. Smith and Sidney Bickford, as defendants.

Fifth. The whole or any part of the printed cases made for use of the court of appeals of the State of New York, on appeal to that court of two actions; one in favor of John T. Davison and others against the City Bank the defendant herein, and the other in favor of Samuel V. Parsons and another against said City Bank.

121   Sixth. The whole or any part of the printed depositions of David Mannering and Delos De Wolf, taken by and before Alfred B. Getty, U. S. commissioner at Oswego, N. Y., on and between the thirtieth day of April and the third day of May, 1870, in certain suits then pending in the circuit court of the United States for the southern district of New York, against John Wilmot, David Dows and others, and Arthur Hughes and others.

And it is stipulated and agreed by and between the attorneys for the respective parties to this action that the portions of the matter aforesaid which may be read as testimony by either party are to have the same force and effect as if testified to by witnesses orally upon the trial or as if read from their respective depositions taken upon commission or de bene esse under the act of Congress, subject, however, to objection by either party, that the same is irrelevant, incompetent, or immaterial.

And it is expressly understood that the defendant is not to be deemed to concede that it had knowledge or notice of any of the transactions mentioned or referred to in said testimony except such transa' as
122   were had by or with the defendant, its officers or agents, or which the testimony shows were brought to the knowledge or notice of the defendant, its officers or agents.

Seventh. The attorneys for the respective parties herein stipulate to admit on the trial of this action that the Milwaukee National Bank, of Wisconsin brought an action of trover against the members of the firm of Hughes, Hickcox & Co., in the fall of 1869, to recover the value of the wheat shipped to that firm on the canal boats A. Post and P. B. Davis in the circuit court of the United States for the southern district of New York, and that such proceedings were had in said action that on the 28th day of July, 1873, a judgment was entered and perfected in favor of the plaintiff and against the defendants therein for $24,865.00 damages, and $792.04 costs, together amounting to $25,657.04. That an appeal from said judgment was taken by the defendants therein to the Supreme Court of the United States, and that pending such appeal the said Hughes, Hickcox & Co. paid to the plaintiff,
123   and said plaintiff received and accepted, the sum of twenty-five thousand dollars, in full satisfaction and settlement and payment of its claim and judgment in said action, together with the costs, and satisfied and discharged said judgment of record, which payment and satisfaction was made and given on the 8th day of March, 1876.

Eighth. Said attorneys also stipulate to admit on the trial of this action that in the fall of 1869 the Milwaukee National Bank of Wisconsin commenced an action of trover in the circuit court of the United States for the southern district of New York against John Wilmot to recover the value of the wheat shipped to him on the canal-boats E. H. Shepard and Moses Melvin, and that such proceedings were had in said action that on the twenty-eighth day of July, 1873, a judgment was entered and perfected against the defendant John Wilmot, and in favor of the plaintiff therein for $24,658.69 damages and $821.40 costs, together amounting to $25,480.09.

124   Ninth. Said attorneys also stipulate to admit on the trial that one G. Woolworth, of Watertown, in the State of New York, received by purchase from A. F. Smith & Co. two thousand and five bushels of the wheat in question in this action, being part of the cargo of the schooner D. G. Fort, which 2,005 bushels of wheat was shipped by A. F. Smith & Co. on the vessel Maid of Judea, and that said Woolworth, on or about the 28th day of February, 1873, paid to the plaintiff, and the plaintiff accepted and received from him, three hundred dollars ($300) in cash and notes in settlement of the plaintiff's claim against him, which notes have been paid.

Tenth. Said attorneys also stipulate to admit on the trial that the firm of Randall & Kenyon received by purchase from A. F. Smith & Co. all the wheat in question, that is to say, all of the wheat of the cargoes of the schooners Atwater and D. G. Fort, excepting the two canal-boat loads shipped to Hughes, Hickcox & Co., the two canal-boat loads shipped to John Wilmot, and the two thousand and five bushels,
125   the cargo of the Maid of Judea, received by Woolworth; and that on or about the 29th day of April, 1876, the said Randall & Kenyon paid to the plaintiff, and the plaintiff accepted and received from them, two thousand four hundred and seventy-three dollars and seventy-three cents ($2,473.73) in settlement of the plaintiff's claim against them.

Eleventh. The attorney for the defendant stipulates and agrees to admit on the trial of this action that the statement of account annexed hereto shows the state of the account of A. F. Smith & Co. with the defendant, and the transactions of A. F. Smith & Co. with the defendant between the 1st day of August, 1869, and the thirtieth day of May, 1870, truly, and as the same appear on the books of account of the defendant, and that the plaintiff may, if so advised, read the same in evidence upon the trial.

Twelfth. The attorney for the plaintiff stipulates and agrees to admit on the trial of this action that in the fall of 1869, and before any 126 suit was commenced by the plaintiff against either John Wilmot or Hughes, Hickcox & Co., and before the actual receipt by Hughes, Hickcox & Co. of the wheat shipped to them on the canal-boats A. Post and P. B. Davis, and before the actual receipt by John Wilmot of the wheat shipped to him on the boats E. H. Shepard and Moses Melvin, it was agreed by and between the plaintiff and said Hughes, Hickcox & Co. and said John Wilmot that the plaintiff would not replevy said wheat but would sue in trover for the value thereof, and in consideration thereof that they, said Hughes, Hickcox & Co. and said John Wilmot, would respectively, on the trial of such actions, admit the receipt by them respectively of such wheat.

Thirteenth. The attorney for the defendant stipulates that he will admit on the trial that from the judgments of the Supreme Court in the suits of John T. Davison and others against The City Bank and Samuel V. Parsons, and another against The City Bank, appeals were taken to the court of appeals of the State of New York, and by that court the said judgments of the supreme court were affirmed with 127 costs.

JUNE 9TH, 1877.

This stipulation is approved by me.

H. M. FINCH.

ALBERTUS PERRY,
Defendant's Attorney.

14th. The defendant also agrees to admit upon the trial aforesaid that upon the appeals to the court of appeals aforesaid in the last two above described actions, in order to perfect said appeals and to stay the collection of the amounts of the several judgments therein, the plaintiff herein caused undertakings in writing by Benjamin E. Bowen and Seabury A. Fuller as sureties to be made in behalf of defendants therein and to be filed and approved according to the rules and practice of said courts, in and by which said sureties undertook and promised, among other things. that if said judgment so appealed from or any part thereof should be affirmed that the appellant therein would pay to the plaintiffs therein the amount directed to be paid by the judgment and all 128 damages awarded against said appellant upon said appeal, and that the said judgments were after argument duly affirmed by the said court of appeals.

And that to protect the said sureties upon said undertakings, the plaintiff in this action paid to the plaintiff in the said actions last above described on February 11th, 1874, as follows: In the Davison case the sum of $2,440.09 ; in the Parsons case the sum of 2,040.93, subject to objection as to relevancy and materiality of the facts stated.

ALBERTUS PERRY,
Def't's Att'y.
GEORGE G. FRENCH,
Pl'ff's Att'y.

129   Said plaintiff, to further maintain the issue on its part, read the following from the printed case prepared for the New York court of appeals in the case of John T. Davison et al. against the City Bank, to wit:

The bill of lading was then read in evidence, and was in the words and figures following, to wit:

MILWAUKEE, *September* 28, 1869.

Shipped in good order and condition, by Mower, Church & Bell, as agents and forwarders, for account and at the risk of whom it may concern, on board the schooner Atwater, whereof J. T. Davison is master, bound from this port for Oswego, N. Y., the following articles as here marked and described, to be delivered in like good order and condition as addressed on the margin, or to his or their assigns or consignees upon paying the freight and charges as noted below, (dangers of navigation, fire and collision excepted.)

And it is agreed between the carriers and shippers and assigns, that in consideration especially of the rate of freight hereon named, the said carriers having supervised the weighing of said cargo inboard, hereby agree that this bill of lading shall be conclusive, as between shippers and assigns and carriers, as to the quantity of cargo to be

130   delivered to consignees at the port of destination (except when grain is heated or heats in transit), and that they will deliver the full quantity herein named, or pay for any part of the cargo not delivered at the current market price; the value thereof to be deducted from the freight money by consignees, if they shall so elect, and thereupon the carrier shall be subrogated to the shippers' and owners' rights of property and action therefor.

And said shippers or owners hereby assign their claim and right of action for such deficiency or deficiencies to the carrier.

In witness whereof the said master of said vessel hath affirmed to bills of lading of this tenor and date, one of which being accomplished the other to stand void.

Acc't T. L. Baker to City Bank, Oswego, N. Y.

. (17,000) seventeen thousand bushels No. two (2) Milwaukee wheat.
Lake freights thirteen (13) cents per bushel to Oswego.
MOWER, CHURCH & BELL.

It was here conceded as a fact that T. L. Baker named in the margin of the bill of lading was cashier of the Milwaukee National Bank

131   of Wisconsin. Upon the face of the bill of lading at the bottom thereof was an order in the words and figures following, to wit:

Deliver to the Corn Exchange Elevator for the account of T. L. Baker, cashier, Milwaukee, subject to the order of the City Bank, Oswego, Oct. 9th, 1869.
D. MANNERING,
Cashier.

It was conceded that David Mannering was in October, 1869, cashier of the City Bank, Oswego, and that he signed the said order. The said order was then read in evidence by the plaintiffs.

There was an endorsement upon the back of said bill of lading, in the words and figures following, to wit:

Received 17,000 bu. fr't, 13c		$2,210 00
Less 45.34 bu. sh't............................	56 96	
" elevating	42 38	
" shoveling	67 81	
P'd captain...................................	2,042 85	

$2,210 00

A. F. SMITH & CO.
F.

It was conceded that A. F. Smith & Co. were in the fall of 1869 proprietors of the Corn Exchange Elevator, and that the signature
132   "A. F. Smith & Co." subscribed to said statement is in the handwriting of one Forsyth, a clerk of A. F. Smith & Co.

The statement on the back of the bill of lading was read in evidence.

JOHN T. DAVISON, called and sworn as a witness on the part of the plaintiffs, testified as follows:

I reside in Buffalo, and did in 1869.

Question. During the season of 1869 who were owners of the schooner S. T. Atwater?

The witness answered: Hosea Rogers, George Hardison, and I owned her. I sailed her as master during the season of 1869.

(The bill of lading in evidence was here shown to the witness.)

I took on board the cargo mentioned in the bill of lading at Milwaukee, on the 28th of September, 1869. I received this bill of lading and signed two or three duplicates. The duplicates were delivered to the shippers. The business between me and the shippers was done by a broker. I took on board the seventeen thousand bushels of wheat and came to Oswego, where I arrived on the 9th of October. On my arrival
133   I went early in the morning to the residence of David Mannering, cashier of the City Bank. Mr. Mannering was not up when I got there, but soon came down, and I presented him the bill of lading. He then wrote this order upon the bottom of the bill of lading, and returned the bill to me.

Question. What did he say, if anything?

Answer. He told me they would pay the freight, meaning the Corn Exchange Elevator. He gave me to understand that.

Question. Do you recall the expression?

Answer. He said, "They will pay the freight," or "they will pay your freight," and handed me back the bill of lading. I went over to the elevator and left the bill of lading at the elevator office; got the vessel ready to commence unloading, and commenced unloading as soon as I could; commenced unloading early in the morning, not far from seven o'clock, I should think. Pretty soon after I commenced unloading I received some money; I don't recollect how much; somewhere from $300 to $500. It might have been over $300. They finished elevating my cargo in the vicinity of four o'clock in the afternoon. I delivered all the grain which I received on board. By the weight of the elevator I was "short" forty-five bushels
134   and 34 pounds. After I had finished elevating I went to the office of A. F. Smith & Co. to settle the freight. I found there some one of the firm of Smith & Co.; I could not say which one of them; it was either Mr. Smith or Mr. Bickford; I recognize him here as Mr. Smith. I do not know Mr. Bickford. I recollect I have see Mr. Forsyth.

Question. What occurred?

Answer. They did not have money to pay the freight; they represented that it was scarce; they went out to see if they could get some, and I went to tow my vessel to another elevator to load a load of barley for Chicago. I returned to Mr. Smith's office after a while; I think it was after five o'clock. I saw Mr. Bickford there then; he is the "Co." of the firm.

(It was here admitted that the firm consists of A. F. Smith and Sidney Bickford.)

Mr. Bickford stated that he had been unable to raise any money; that he had been to several banks; among the rest of the banks he had been to the City Bank, and he could not get any money. He said he would go down north from his office and see if he could raise any. He was gone half an hour, I should think. He returned and was unable to get any money.

Question. What occurred?

135   Answer. He returned unable to get any money, and he settled the freight by giving checks. He gave me several checks for small amounts to pay my bills in Oswego; several small checks on banks in Oswego; then he gave me these New York checks. I told him I would rather have bank exchange on New York. He could not give me anything else; and he said that these would be good after I had signed them, and went on with the settlement.

Four checks were here exhibited to the witness, who identified them as the checks given to witness by A. F. Smith & Co., and he testified that the checks were, in fact, signed by Mr. Bickford.

The checks were read in evidence and were in the words and figures following, to wit:

$400.   No. 1719.

COMMISSION HOUSE OF A. F. SMITH & CO.,
Oswego, N. Y., Oct. 9, 1869.

Pay to the order of Capt. Jno. T. Davison four hundred dollars.

A. F. SMITH & CO.

To the Fourth National Bank, New York.

(Endorsed:)
Pay Hosea Rogers, esq., of Rochester, N. Y.

JNO. T. DAVISON.

Pay Stettheimer, Tone & Co., or order.

136   HOSEA ROGERS.

Pay Importers and Traders' National Bank or order.

STETTHEIMER, TONE & CO.

$400.   No. 1720.

COMMISSION HOUSE OF A. F. SMITH & CO.,
Oswego, N. Y., Oct. 9, 1869.

Pay to the order of Capt. Jno. T. Davison four hundred dollars.

A. F. SMITH & CO.

To the Fourth National Bank, New York.

(Endorsed:)
Pay to C. G. Flint, esq., or order.

JNO. T. DAVISON.
C. G. FLINT.

Pay to H. F. Vail, esq., or order.

C. P. LEE, Secretary.

$352 $\frac{43}{100}$. No. 1721.

COMMISSION HOUSE OF A. F. SMITH & CO.,
Oswego, N. Y., Oct. 9, 1869.

Pay to order of Capt. Jno. T. Davison three hundred fifty-two $\frac{43}{100}$ dollars.

A. F. SMITH & CO.

To the Fourth National Bank, New York.

(Endorsed :)
    Pay C. G. Flint, esq., or order.

137   JNO. T. DAVISON.
                                                             C. G. FLINT.

Pay to H. F. Vail, esq.

                                                             C. P. LEE, *Sec'y.*

$352.$\frac{42}{100}$. No. 1722.

COMMISSION HOUSE OF A. F. SMITH & CO.,
Oswego, N. Y., Oct. 9, 1869.

Pay to the order of Capt. Jno. T. Davison three hundred fifty two $\frac{42}{100}$ dollars.

A. F. SMITH & CO.

To the Fourth National Bank, New York.

(Endorsed :)
Pay to C. G. Flint, esq., or order.

                                                             JNO. T. DAVISON.
                                                             C. G. FLINT.

Pay to H. F. Vail, esq.

                                                             C. P. LEE, *Sec'y.*

(A written statement was here shown to the witness.)
I signed this statement. It was made there in the office.
The statement was read in evidence, and was in the words and figures following, to wit:

OSWEGO, *Oct.* 9, '69.

Rec'd per B. S. sch'r Atwater, Davison, master, Milwaukee, Sept. 28. Shipped by Mower, Church & Bell.

17,000 bus. wheat, frt. 13 c		$2,210 00
138 Less 45 $\frac{33}{100}$ bus. sh't @ 1.25	56 96	
" elevating	42 38	
Less shoveling	67 80	
P'd captain	2,042 85	
		$2,210 00

Received freight as above.
    (Signed)   JNO. T. DAVISON.

My bill of lading was returned to me with the statement endorsed upon the back of it signed " A. F. Smith & Co."
This transaction was closed at the office close on to six o'clock I should think. It was Saturday evening. The last mail leaving Oswego that day had left when I got to the post-office. I went aboard the vessel and wrote letters enclosing these checks, and when I got to the post-office the mail had gone.

It was conceded that the mail closed at about five o'clock p. m., an hour before the last train left Oswego.

There was nothing said between me and A. F. Smith & Co. as to my taking these checks absolutely.

Question by the court. What was said about the checks? Anything about their having funds?

Answer. No, sir.

139   Question by the court. About their having funds in New York?

Answer. I supposed they had funds there. Mr. Bickford said these checks would be good when I signed them. I took the checks at once on board of the vessel, and sent one of them to Mr. Hosea Rogers and the balance to my father-in-law. I sent one of the four hundred dollar checks by mail to Hosea Rogers at Rochester. I deposited it in the office Saturday night after six o'clock. I deposited the other three checks at the same time with the letter to my father-in-law at Buffalo (whose name is C. G. Flint), with orders to send them at once for collection. I never received from any source any portion of this balance of $1,504.85.

It was here conceded that the letter addressed to Hosea Rogers, at Rochester, reached him on the 12th of October, and that the check enclosed in it was deposited by Mr. Rogers with Stettheimer, Tone & Co., bankers, at Rochester, on the 12th of October, 1869, but too late to leave the bank by the mail of that day; that Stettheimer, Tone & Co. sent the check by mail, on the 13th of October, to the Importers and Traders' National Bank, New York, for collection; that on the 16th

146   of October this check was presented at the Fourth National Bank, in the city of New York, for payment, and payment was demanded and refused; that the certificate attached to the check shows that it was presented by a notary at the request of the Importers & Traders' National Bank; that a notice of protest for non-payment, dated New York, October 16, 1869, was sent to Hosea Rogers.

The witness further testified: I received notice of protest on each one of the checks.

It was also conceded that the other three checks were received by Mr. C. G. Flint, at Buffalo, on the 12th of October, 1869, and were deposited by him with the Erie County Savings Bank; that on the same day they were sent forward to New York for collection; that on the 14th of October they were presented at the Fourth National Bank in the city of New York for payment, and payment was demanded and refused; that they were protested for non-payment, and notice thereof was given to the endorsers.

Three of these checks were returned to me. The fourth was sent to my attorney, Mr. Perry, at Oswego. On Monday morning, one

141   week from the Monday next after the day I received the checks from A. F. Smith & Co., I called at the City Bank on this subject. I went to the bank and demanded my freight, and told them that Mr. Smith's checks had been protested. I saw Mr. Mannering. I had three of the checks with me at the time; the other one had not yet been received from Mr. Rogers. They did not pay the freight; they did give me a decided answer the first or second time I went there, and along about noon they said they would not pay it.

On cross examination by defendant's counsel, this witness testified: I have never delivered any other cargo than this to the Corn Exchange elevator. I was not informed as to this cargo that A. F. Smith & Co. were the owners of it, nor that they were to have it.

A statement of the account of A. F. Smith & Co. with the Fourth National Bank of New York, certified by T. E. Lathrop, assistant cashier, was here produced by the plaintiff's counsel.

It was conceded that the statement showed correctly how their account stood on the books of that bank on the several days mentioned in the statement. The statement was here read in evidence, and was in the words and figures following, to wit:

142   *A. F. Smith & Co., Oswego, in account with Fourth National Bank, N. Y.*

Oct. 9, 1869.	Balance		$10,283 47
Oct. 11.	Paid accept'ce of Taylor Sons		10,173 25
" 11.	Balance		120 22
" 12.	Paid pro. fee	1 76	
	Draft	4 00	5 76
" 12.	Balance		114 46
" 13.	"		114 46
" 14.	"		114 46
" 15.	"		114 46
" 16.	"		114 46
1870.			
March 24.	Paid draft		100 00
" "	Balance		14 46
Aug. 3.	Paid draft		8 47
	Balance from Aug. 3 to 29		$5 99

I certify that the above is a true copy of the account and balance on the days stated of A. F. Smith & Co., as shown by the books of this bank.

T. E. LATHROP,
A. Cas. 4 Nat. B'k, N. Y.

Aug. 29, 1870.

The witness further testified: I got to Oswego very soon after daylight Saturday morning, and tied up my vessel a little below the 143   Corn Exchange elevator. I hired a tug to get to the elevator.

ANANIAS F. SMITH was sworn as a witness on behalf of the defendants, and testified as follows:

I am one of the firm of A. F. Smith and Co. I remember this cargo of wheat which has been testified of.

Question. Whose wheat was it?

The firm of A. F. Smith & Co. purchased it, or ordered it purchased.

Question. From whom was it purchased?

Answer. Mower, Church & Bell. It was purchased by them for us.

Question. Did The City Bank, the defendant in this suit, have any interest in this wheat, to your knowledge?

Answer. No, sir.

Question by the court. You say the wheat was purchased on your account. Was the wheat drawn against by the shippers?

Answer. Yes, sir; we paid by our acceptance. They drew one sight draft and one time draft, and they were accepted by us and held by The City Bank.

By the court. Were those drafts paid at the time the wheat arrived at Oswego?

Answer. No, sir; I suppose they were drawn through The City Bank.

By the court. Do you know how the wheat came to be shipped to The City Bank?

144   Answer. We supposed it was done to procure our acceptance.

By the court. Probably the consignment was made to The City Bank to protect the drafts?

The witness answered: "Yes, sir."

He further testified: I do not remember of being on the dock when the cargo was being received; I may have been. I do not remember when the captain was there. I do not remember any conversation with him. I may have been there. At that time I understood our account to be good in New York. I was good.

Question. Look at this bank account, and explain what that ten thousand dollar item is in your account.

Answer. This ten thousand dollars of Taylor and Sons was an acceptance of theirs which had been discounted by us, and happening to fall due about this time, and Taylor and Sons not paying it, it was charged to us. Taylor & Sons afterwards paid it to Smith, Wemple & Co., of Albany. It was not returned as soon as it might have been. I do not remember the date of the payment of this acceptance by Taylor & Sons.

I cannot say; Mr. Bickford attended to that matter himself. He
145   attended to the inside matters. The acceptance was paid with
our funds, and no funds were afterwards put in the bank to replace them. I cannot give the amounts of the time draft and the sight draft.

It was conceded that the sight draft was for $5,085.43, and the time draft was for $15,000 at thirty days.

On cross-examination by plaintiffs' counsel, the witness testified: The sight draft was handed in to us by The City Bank. They also presented the time draft for acceptance. I do not know how long before the arrival of this cargo the sight draft was paid; perhaps twelve days; I am not certain. When the cargo arrived it was placed in the Corn Exchange elevator. The time draft had not then matured. That was never paid. I have heard since that it was held by The City Bank. The firm of A. F. Smith & Co. failed on the 16th of October, 1869. We then suspended, and have not resumed payment since. The wheat was sold; some of it was sent to New York by us on our own account. We sold it, before we failed, to various parties. We got money for the
wheat. There is a suit pending for the value of that wheat brought
146   by the Milwaukee National Bank of Wisconsin; an action of
trover to recover the value of this cargo of wheat. That suit has not been determined.

On being re-examined by defendant's counsel, the witnessed testified: I think there was no other receipt ever given by our firm for this wheat except the one on the back of the bill of lading.

JOHN H. FORSYTH, being sworn as a witness on behalf of the defendant, testified as follows:

In October, 1869, I was clerk and bookkeeper of A. F. Smith & Co.

The bill of lading in evidence was here shown to the witness, and he testified: I drew the receipt on the back of the bill of lading which I hold in my hand. It was dated October 9th. I could not say what took place in reference to the payment of the freight. I don't think I paid the freight on that. I think I remember the captain being in the office. I do not remember of anything being said to the captain about the wheat belonging to A. F. Smith & Co. I think I left it for Mr. Bickford to

pay the freight. I signed the receipt. There was no objection, in my
hearing, to the taking of the checks. Mr. Bickford is not present.
147   His wife was taken suddenly ill, and he could not come. It was
my business to make up statements for A. F. Smith & Co. I also
drew the receipt. I usually paid the freight. I did not do it this time.
I have no recollection of the captain having been there with a cargo before this.

On cross-examination the witness testified: I presume the captain
took the bill of lading away with him when he left.

DAVID MANNERING, being duly sworn on behalf   the defendant, testified as follows:

I am cashier of the City Bank, and reside in Oswego. I signed the
order which is written upon the foot of the bill of lading in this case;
that is, the order to deliver the cargo. The City Bank had no pecuniary
interest in this cargo of wheat.

Question. At the time the vessel arrived there with the cargo, had
the City Bank any funds for the payment of the freight?

Answer. It had no funds to pay freight.

On being cross-examined by plaintiff's counsel, the witness testified:
The City Bank had no funds belonging to the Milwaukee National Bank
of Wisconsin at the time of the arrival of this vessel. They had funds
a few days after that, more than enough to pay the freight on this and
the schooner Forts' cargo.

148   Question. Has the City Bank now funds belonging to the Milwaukee National Bank of Wisconsin, which it retains as indemnity against this suit?

Answer. Yes, sir; it has. The City Bank received a bill of lading of
this wheat from the Milwaukee National Bank of Wisconsin before the
arrival of the vessel. That bill of lading came to the City Bank accompanied by two drafts; one was a sight draft and the other was a time
draft. I have a letter which will tell me the amounts.

The witness produced the letter and the same was read in evidence.

[E. Cramer, president; S. L. Baker, cashier. Milwaukee National Bank successor to
the State Bank of Wisconsin, organized 1853.]

MILWAUKEE, *Sept.* 29, 1869.

D. MANNERING, Esq., *Cas.*:

DEAR SIR: I enclose for collection and remittance to Nat. Park Bank,
N. Y., bills as stated below:

A. F. Smith & Co., sight.. $5,085 43
    "   "   30th Oct...................................... $15,000
149   B. L. schooner Atwater, 17,000 bushels 2 wheat. Cer. Ætna
Ins. Co., $11,250; Home Ins. Co., $10,000. Weight and inspection.
Please hold above cert'f's insurance for arrival of vessel, and on the
wheat going into store please have it insured for enough to cover draft.
On payment of the drafts you will please deliver the cargo to order of
Messrs. Smith & Co. If not paid, please hold and advise me by tele-
graph. Messrs. Smith & Co. will pay all expenses.

Truly, yours,

S. L. BAKER, *Cas.*

The City Bank never gave any order for the disposition of this wheat
after it was put in the Corn Exchange Elevator. It was disposed of with-

out their knowledge. The sight draft referred to in that letter was paid, and the time draft was never paid.

On being re-examined by defendant's counsel, the witness testified: I first learned that this wheat had gone from the warehouse on the afternoon of Saturday, the 16th of October. The money I spoke of as received afterward was part of the proceeds of another cargo of wheat; no part of it was the proceeds of this cargo. It was never put into my hands for the purpose of paying any part of this freight.

150

On further cross-examination by plaintiffs' counsel, the witness testified: I think A. F. Smith & Co. failed on the 16th of October, 1869.

ANANIAS F. SMITH was recalled by the plaintiffs and testified:

The Corn Exchange Elevator is located in the harbor of Oswego; it is capable of storing 250,000 bushels of grain. In 1869 that elevator was used by A. F. Smith & Co. for storing grain for others for hire, and for storing grain purchased by themselves. It was used as a warehouse.

Question. Did you receive notice of protest of these checks in due course of mail?

Answer. I have no doubt we did. Mr. Bickford attended to that part of the business.

On cross-examination by defendants' counsel, the witness testified: A part of the business of an elevator is what is called spouting, which is transferring the cargoes of vessels into canal boats. I cannot say whether or not this cargo was spouted directly into a canal boat. The books will show. If spouted, it would not be left in the elevator. I cannot say how soon after this wheat arrived it was shipped by us to New York. The books will show. It is very possible it was spouted right into a canal boat; that was our general course of business.

151

The plaintiffs here offered to surrender the four checks in evidence to whoever might be entitled to them.

The plaintiffs then rested their case.

JOHN T. DAVISON was recalled by the defendant, and testified:

Question. Do you know whether any part of this wheat was spouted?

Answer. They loaded a canal-boat at the same time our vessel was being unloaded. A canal-boat load would be about six or seven thousand bushels. I think only one canal boat was loaded while my vessel was being unloaded. I cannot say during what part of the unloading it was. The checks were received after my vessel was unloaded.

On cross-examination by plaintiffs' counsel, the witness testified: I have no knowledge where the wheat which went into the canal-boat came from. I loaded my vessel for Chicago on Saturday night, and left Oswego the same night. I went up the lake with my vessel. After leaving the Welland Canal, I met a violent gale of wind on the lake. I ran back to Port Colburn, and went to Buffalo and got new sails, where I received notice of this protest. I then came directly back to Oswego.

152

The testimony was here closed.

Thereupon the court directed the jury to find a verdict for the plaintiffs for the sum of $1,600.13, subject to the opinion of the court at general term, and a verdict was found and entered accordingly.

LEROY MORGAN,
Justice Supreme Court.

153 And said plaintiff, to further maintain the issue on its part, called as a witness DELOS DE WOLF, who, being duly sworn, testified

that he was the president of the City Bank in October, 1867, and been for twelve years up to this time; that D. Mannering was its cashier and his brother-in law; that there are four elevators in Oswego, and three or four that are used as mills; that such was the fact in 1869; that they are fitted up with bins as warehouses usually are—making seven or eight elevators in all; that the city of Oswego is divided by a river; that elevators are on east side of the river, that is, one elevator is on the west side, and the others on the east side; the elevators on the east side are along the dock adjoining the Corn Exchange Elevator: the largest elevator is on the west side; that he had known A. F. Smith before he came to Oswego slightly, had a passing acquaintance with him, and knew he was a business man at Cape Vincent; he came to Oswego in 1868 and commenced business that year with defendant; he

154   kept a large balance with the bank and never borrowed very much money; he borrowed money in 1869 on his own note and on drafts on New York; the account annexed to stipulation states what it was after the first of August, 1869; he had no notes at the bank upon which he was indebted on the first day of September, 1869; he was a dealer in grain, shipper, warehouseman; did not sell to him any interest in the Corn Exchange Elevator; he owned an interest in that elevator; I think Mr. Winslow, president of the Merchants' Bank of Watertown. owned the elevator with him; I owned a one-sixth interest in the elevator; I did not know whether or not Smith had paid for an interest in the elevator; I suppose that he had; I know Smith purchased grain at times at the West on sight and time drafts; I suppose I first knew when Smith was receiving grain against which drafts were drawn in the month of Sept., 1869, when we received the bills of lading from the plaintiff; I saw the drafts and bills of lading sent by the plaintiff; I think I did not know of the shipments before receipt of the bills of lading;

155   I think I had never had any conversation with Smith in relation to receiving grain from the West; am quite sure I did not. The first I knew of these two cargoes was when the bills of lading came. I presume I talked with Mannering what to do with the bills of lading. I presume I gave him the form of the order to put on the captain's bill of lading; it was a form we had used a great while. I presume some time I gave him the form, and perhaps used it myself. I did not give Mr. Mannering directions, when the bill of lading came into the bank, and the captains called for their order, that he was to endorse that form of order on the captains' bill of lading. I was not there then. I did not see Mannering until it was all done. I don't know as I gave Mannering any instructions. I think sometimes I drew the form of the order to put the grain in the elevator. We had considerable grain first and last. I think that, likely, was the form of the order I used when I was cashier before he was. I don't know as I told Mannering anything; don't think I did. I said I had some conversation with Mannering

156   about the orders. I don't recollect I did about this. I don't think I went to the Corn Exchange Elevator at any time after the orders were given to see whether the grain was in the elevator. I think the bank did not take any warehouse receipts for these cargoes. I know of the firm of Smith, Wemple & Co.

Question. Do you know who compose that firm?

I understood from A. F. Smith, his brother. I see by the testimony I did not know who they were. I think a man by the name of Wemple and another man were the firm. I did not know much about the firm; it was located at Albany. They were dealers in grain, hops and barley. I did not understand from A. F. Smith he was a member of that firm until after he failed. I know nothing of the pecuniary responsibility of the firm of Smith, Wemple & Co., except what Smith told me; he told me they were good. I knew very little about their responsibility; they stood well in Albany, our correspondent advised us. I had no idea of the extent of the business of A. F. Smith & Co. with Smith, Wemple & Co., except what went through the bank. I knew Edson, of the firm of Franklin, Edson & Co.; the firm was located in New York; they were grain dealers; I always had a good report of them. We did a good deal of business with him before he went to New York and afterward. The bank keeps a day-book, journal, ledger, discount-book, note-book, and a tickler, as we call it—a collection register. When A. F. Smith came to Oswego, he was reported to have $40,000 to $50,000 in capital. I do not remember how much he put into our bank on deposit when he first came there. I should not wonder if he put in $5,000 or—do not recollect amount; could not tell within $5,000. He commenced business in Oswego in spring of 1868. By the account annexed to stipulation, it appears that on the first day of August, 1869, Smith had a credit in our bank of $317.67. I do not know on whom the check of $7,136.24, of August 3rd, was drawn. I do not know whether it was drawn on a bank in New York. He had a good many accounts. I think he drew checks on the Ninth National and on the Fourth National of New York. I guess he used to draw on the First National, at our place, some checks, and some on Norris Winslow' bank at Watertown. I have no recollection of seeing checks on Winslow's bank. I cannot tell on whom the next check, drawn August 7th, for $15,952.24, was drawn. Smith used to have a good deal of sight-paper on somebody in N. Y. This item might have been two or three checks. The item says checks; it is very likely it was not all one check. My office is in the bank, and I am there most of the time when at home and generally know what is going on, particularly in the way of discounting paper. I generally look after that. I do not know upon what bank or banks the checks under dates of August 12th, 13th, 17th, and 19th were drawn. The bank received no security for the draft mentioned in the account as of the date of August 21st, 1869, on Smith, Wemple & Co. at 20 days, for $5,000.00. The bank took the draft as it is entered in the account. I do say that as president of the bank I made that discount of $5,000.00 without knowing very much about the pecuniary responsibility of Smith, Wemple & Co. I did it on the responsibility of A. F. Smith & Co. The entry on the 24th, Smith, Wemple & Co., on John Taylor & Sons, 60 days from date, due October 16th, $10,250, was drawn, I think, to the order of A. F. Smith & Co. John Taylor and Sons were brewers at Albany. I do not know upon whom the checks under date of August 26th, amounting in the aggregate to $12,000, were drawn; don't think they were drawn on Smith, Wemple & Co.; have no recollection of sight paper on them; my best recollection is, that all paper on them was time paper. Franklin, Edson & Co. were a commission house in N. Y. City. I have known them a long time. The draft of 10,495.80 was not accepted when we discounted it I presume. I presume it was afterward accepted. Smith & Co. were the drawers of the draft of the date of Sept. 2d, on Smith, Wemple & Co., at fifteen days from date, for $7,000.00. The draft of Sept. 4th of A. F. Smith & Co., on Franklin, Edson & Co., for $5,449.56, was undoubtedly accepted, but not at the time we discounted it. I think a bill of lading accompanied these drafts. There was no security to the drafts of Smith, Wemple & Co. on John Taylor & Sons. They were good enough. I think that draft was accepted before

we discounted it. I did not know that John Taylor & Sons did not pay that draft. The draft on Franklin, Edson & Co. of Sept. 4th, for 5,449.50, was discounted for benefit of A. F. Smith & Co. I presume se-
160 curity accompanied that draft. I think we had no security for the draft of A. F. Smith & Co. on Smith, Wemple & Co., of the date of the 23d of Sept., for $5,000.00. I did not know, until after their failure, that A. F. Smith & Co. were having cargoes of wheat purchased at the West with the drafts and bills of lading sent to the Merchants' Bank at Watertown, N. Y. I think we took no check from Smith on Norris Winslow or the Merchants' Bank. I first heard of A. F. Smith & Co.'s failure Saturday afternoon, between 5 and 6 o'clock, of the 16th of October; I think likely I saw A. F. Smith between the date of the receipt of the drafts and bills of lading and their failure. He had been in the bank. I do not know what he came there for, unless he brought over the drafts accepted. I had no conversation with him about the failure prior to the failure; never dreamed of it or heard of it until that afternoon. Smith told me he had stopped; he said he had to stop. I asked him about the wheat. He said he did not want to say anything; his counsel advised him not to say anything; that he had telegraphed for all of the parties to come there. I do not think he told me
161 on the 16th he had shipped the wheat. I sent a man to the ele-
vator, and sent for Smith. I do not think I was in the elevator after the order was given to the captains, and before the 16th. I made no inquiries in relation to the whereabouts of the wheat from the date of the order until the day of the failure, and I presume Mr. Mannering did not. I sent Judge Churchill over to the elevator to see Smith. I suppose he was Smith's attorney, and he was ours, too. We could not find the wheat until we learned the boats; Smith would not tell us where they were; he said he would when the people from New York and Milwaukee got there. I inquired of several of the forwarding men what boats had gone, but I could not identify the wheat. I don't remember how many boat-loads I found he had shipped. I had no diffi-
culty with Smith; had been on friendly terms with him to the 16th of October. The plaintiff had him arrested in Oswego. I did not go on his bond. My relations with Smith were such that I dared to talk with him about the shipment of the wheat; he would not then tell me anything about the shipment of the wheat; his counsel advised him not to
do so. I did not ask any employee of the elevator where the
162 wheat was. I learned through Churchill it was shipped out. I
did not go to the elevator; I learned the situation well enough. Smith and Bickford were not there. I do not know that any great cold-
ness existed between Smith and me after the 16th. The bank account is a correct statement from our ledger, and shows the state of account as kept. I cannot tell on whom the checks were drawn on the 9th of October, aggregating $12,675, nor the checks of $5,100.00 deposited Octo-
ber 4th, nor the checks deposited on the 14th of October, two days be-
fore the failure, of $9,876.67. I do not recollect about that; I do not think I knew; I might have known. I do not know where the checks are. They were other people's checks, and I did not of course give them up to Smith. I saw Mr. Hayden at the bank. He came to the bank and demanded the wheat; he said they should sue us for it. I told him we stored it for their account and they run it off; that I had no doubt they could find it; that Smith had agreed to give the names of the boats it was shipped on. The conversation was short; the young man
163 was quite set up, I thought, with his position; he was going to
do something and I let him talk. I told him I could not give him

the wheat; he was a young man; I told him I was willing to do anything I could for him, and I had no doubt they would tell where the
wheat was, for Smith said he should, and he did; he learned right away
where the wheat was. I first knew that Winslow had received bills of
lading on Monday; perhaps Judge Churchill told me on Saturday. I
leased the elevator to Smith; he was owing me rent for it when he failed,
some $500.00 or $600.00; part of it was due. It has never been paid.
I leased my one-sixth of it.

Cross examined:

The elevator is built with bins. You can't see much by looking into
the door. It is all bins, holding from 12 to 15,000 bushels. All the
grain comes in at the top and goes out at the bottom of the bins,
and when it comes out it is elevated again by a belt and spouted into
the weigh hopper. The elevator is about 100 feet high from the water.
The wheat is taken from the vessel by the elevator, the leg of the elevator let down from the elevator into the hold of the vessel. This leg
is an en'less belt with tin cups upon it. The wheat is carried up
164   in these cups and carried into the warehouse, then weighed and
then carried to the different bins. If the bins are full to the top
you can see the wheat, but if they are not full or much below the top,
you cannot, because it is dark. If we had gone to the elevator and
looked into the bins we could not have told whether the grain was
wheat or not. The bins must be 60 or 75 feet deep. The wheat is
drawn out of the bin at the bottom by opening a slide. The balance of
account of A. F. Smith & Co., in 1868, with our bank was from 20,000
to $75,000.00. It was not so much in 1869. They drew out freely; did
not have much balance; usually was not as much business. The reputation of A. F. Smith & Co. for pecuniary responsibility in 1868, and
up to 1869, was good. Their reputation during that time for commercial integrity was as good as any one in town. The City Bank had no
elevator or place for storage of grain, and never had. None of the banks
had, at any time, had any elevator, warehouse, or place for the storage
of grain.

And thereupon said defendant, by its counsel, propounded the following question : When grain has been consigned to banks at
165   Oswego, and drafts upon time drawn against the grain have
been sent to such bank for collection, with instructions to hold
the grain till the payment of such drafts, what has been the usual
course of action of banks at Oswego ?

To which said question said plaintiff, by its counsel, did then and
there object as irrelevant and incompetent, which said objection was
then and there overruled, and the question allowed, and to which said
ruling said plaintiff, by his said counsel, did then and there except, and
the witness answered: "It has always been ordered into the warehouse of the party drawn upon by the party receiving it, and stored for
the party sending it, subject to the order of the bank having the drafts,
if the party had a warehouse; such was the usage of the banks in Oswego in 1869, and prior to that time. Such has been the custom for
twenty years, and I do not know of any departure from it. We have
always done so, stored for the account of the party sending it, subject
to our order. (All of the above testimony as to the usage was objected
by plaintiff as irrelevant and incompetent. Objection overruled and
testimony allowed, and to which ruling plaintiff, by his coun-
166   sel, did then and there except.) I have dealt in grain. I put
three cargoes into the Corn Exchange elevator in 1868. I did not

have any in 1869. I recollect the receipt of the letters of T. L. Baker, cashier, enclosing drafts and bills of lading of the cargoes in question. I showed the letters to Smith at the bank. I think he brought back the acceptances. When drafts with bills of lading enclosed, as were these, are sent to Oswego banks, they are sent over to the parties upon whom drawn for payment of the sight and acceptance of the time drafts, and for examination by the parties. Generally all of the papers are sent in the morning, and we get them back in the evening. That was done in this case with the consignments of the Atwater and the Fort. The bank had the bills of lading after the acceptance. I did not, and no officer of the City Bank gave Smith & Co. any order or permission to sell, ship, or deliver from the elevator any portion of the cargoes of the Atwater and Fort. I had no knowledge or information that A. F. Smith & Co. had before this time sold or shipped grain which had been stored in this elevator for the account of the owner, and subject to the order of a bank before payment of the time drafts. I had not, and no officer of the bank, to my knowledge, ever given A. F. Smith & Co. permission to sell or ship grain thus stored until payment of the drafts. I first learned A. F. Smith & Co. claimed the right to do so after this failure. When the drafts were paid, they, with the bill of lading, certificate of inspection, insurance policies, were delivered to the party. The City Bank took warehouse receipts from A. F. Smith & Co. on two cargoes sent before these. The cargoes were divided. We were ordered to deliver one-half of the cargo when one draft was paid. There were two drafts made, and Smith suggested they send over the warehouse receipts for it, so that when they paid one draft they could get up a receipt. This was the only occasion I recollect of taking warehouse receipts. They were the cargoes of the Phalorope and Gerritt Smith. I have the letters of instructions in these cases. They read as follows:

EXHIBIT A.

MILWAUKEE, *July* 10*th*, 1869.

DAVID MANNERING, ESQ., *Cas.*:

168   DEAR SIR: I enclose for collection and remittance to Nat. Park Bank, N.Y., bills as stated below. Your favor of   . with enclosure, received:

A. F. Smith & Co., sight 1,368 60
"   August 11 8,900
"   "   26 8,900

B. L. schr. Gerritt Smith, 15,336$\frac{50}{60}$ bushels No. 1 Milwaukee wheat.

Certificate Ætna Insurance Co 12,950
"   Home   "   "   10,000
"   of weight inspection.

On payment draft 8,900, due 11 August, please deliver one-half the cargo to A. F. Smith & Co.; and on payment draft 8,900 due 26 August deliver the other half. Please hold the enclosed insurance certificates, and on the wheat going into store have it insured sufficient to cover drafts, holding the control of it yourself. Messrs. Smith & Co. will pay all expenses.

Truly yours,

T. L. BAKER, *Cas.*

EXHIBIT B.

MILWAUKEE, *Sept.* 8, 1869.

D. MANNERING, Esq., *Cas.*:

169   DEAR SIR: I enclose for collection and remittance to Nat. Park Bank, N. Y., bills as stated below.

On payment of the first draft please deliver one-half the cargo to Messrs. Smith & Co., the balance on payment of the other.

Please hold the certificate of insurance enclosed, and on the wheat going into warehouse please have it insured enough to cover the drafts. Messrs. Smith & Co. will pay all expenses.

Truly yours,

T. L. BAKER, *Cas.*

A. F. Smith & Co., 10 Oct. 9,500
  "   25 "   9,500

B. L. schr. Phalarope, 16,258.35 bushels 1 wheat.

Cer. Northwest Nat. Ins. Co. 22,762
  " inspection & weight.

The draft sent you yesterday on Smith & Co., 3,470.90, was for margins on this cargo, and unless paid you will please hold the wheat.

170   We were never instructed in such cases to take warehouse receipts, and never did except in these two cases. Our bank has furnished to other parties money to buy wheat, and secured itself by the bills of lading consigning the property to us. It would be consigned to the bank, to me as president, or to Mr. Mannering as cashier. We would advance the money to an agent of the party for whom the property was bought. He would be in Canada or Chicago. We would send the money to an agent in whom we had confidence to buy the property for these parties. The property would be sent forward on account and in care of the City Bank, and the drafts and bills of lading sent to us. In such cases we have put the property on arrival in the warehouse of the party for whom it was really purchased—the drawee of the drafts. It would be stored under an order, stored with him subject to our order for account of the party sending drafts.

Redirect:

Cannot tell how many bins are in Corn Exchange elevator. It is rated for 250,000 bushels. It may be the bins hold 4,500 bushels.

171   When a vessel is to be unloaded at the elevator it is hauled up alongside of the dock. What they call the leg of the elevator is passed into the hold of the vessel. This encloses an endless belt with tin scoops on it. The machinery of the elevator carries these scoops to the weigh room at the top of the elevator. The wheat is there weighed in drafts of sixty bushels, and if going into store it is conveyed from its weigh-hopper to the distributing bin and distributed into the bins. If the grain is to be discharged into a canal-boat the boat lays alongside the dock and a spout passes from the elevator to the canal-boat. Where the testimony speaks of " spouting " the wheat, it means, I suppose, that it has gone into the weigh-hopper, and from there into the canal-boat without going into separate bins. By putting head out of the window of the boat can see grain being discharged from the elevator into a canal-boat. I know they keep books in an elevator. I never examined the books of the elevator to see how A. F. Smith & Co. entered these car-

goes. I suppose that under such an order as was given in these cases the cargoes would be entered as they were ordered to be. I did
172   suppose that in this case under the order on the captain's bill of lading that Smith & Co. would enter the cargoes on their books to the account of the Milwaukee Bank. Of course I did not take the trouble to see how they entered it because they run it off. I never examined the insurance certificate given to Mannering. I did not know at the time Mannering asked for that certificate that the wheat was being spouted. I had no idea of it more than you. If we had, I think we should have stopped him. I am told that in all of the elevators in Oswego they keep a receiving and delivering tally-book. The receiving tally-book contains entries of the cargo received, and the delivery-book will undoubtedly show the delivery.

Recross:

The bank did not to my knowledge receive a dollar of the proceeds of the sales of the Atwater and D. G. Fort cargoes.

The following testimony from the printed case prepared for the New York court of appeals in the suit of Samuel V. Parsons et al. against the City Bank was read. The testimony thus read is the same as that in the case of John T. Davison et al. vs. City Bank, to wit, all
173   except the testimony of Captain Davison and the testimony of Captain Holland hereinafter set out.

174, 175   Said plaintiff further read in evidence the testimony of Myron M. Holland, captain of the D. G. Fort, as follows:

MYRON M. HOLLAND, being duly sworn on behalf of the plaintiffs, testified as follows:

I was master of the D. G. Fort during the season of 1869. I received on board of that schooner at Milwaukee this cargo of wheat at the date of the bill of lading and brought it to Oswego, where I arrived on the 9th day of October, 1869, at about 6 o'clock in the forenoon of that day.

Right away after arriving, I reported my arrival to Mr. Mannering at his house. I did not take the bill of lading with me at that time. I saw him and told him that the Fort had arrived there with a cargo of wheat for the City Bank. He said, "All right; deliver it to the Corn Exchange Elevator." I went and got my vessel as near as I could to the Corn Exchange Elevator. The schooner Atwater had got there a little ahead of me. After I had got my vessel as near as I could I went over to the City Bank with my bill of lading and presented it to Mr. Mannering. He then wrote and signed that order on the bottom of the bill, and returned the bill of lading to me. He told me they would pay the
176   freight. I kept the bill of lading in my pocket until after I was unloaded. I unloaded at the Corn Exchange Elevator and delivered to the elevator all the wheat which I received at Milwaukee. My vessel was discharged along in the night of Saturday. I cannot tell the hour; somewhere from twelve to two o'clock. I think I did not receive any money before my vessel was unloaded. On Monday I went to the office of A. F. Smith & Co. It was about the middle of the day. It may have been a little before or a little after 12 o'clock. I cannot say exactly what time it was. I took the bill of lading with me. The memorandum on the back of the bill was made there at that time by A. F. Smith & Co. I saw Mr. Smith and presented him the bill of lading. He said, "How do you want your freight paid?" I told him I wanted the currency. He says, "Currency is scarce here. It is impossible to get cur-

rency. I will go out and see what I can do for you." He went out and was gone about three-quarters of an hour. He came back and says, "I will give you a check for $1,200, and the balance in currency; that is the best I can do."

A check for $1,200, payable to the order of S. V. Parsons, was exhibited to the witness, who testified: Mr. Smith gave me this check at that time.

177   The check was here read in evidence, and was in the words and figures following, to wit:

$1,200. No. 1724.

COMMISSION HOUSE OF A. F. SMITH & CO.,
Oswego, N. Y., Oct. 11th, 1869.

Pay to the order of S. V. Parsons twelve hundred dollars.

A. F. SMITH & CO.

To the Fourth National Bank, New York.

(Endorsed:) S. V. Parsons.

Pay George I. Seney, cashier, or order, for collection or account of Bank of Attica.

CHAS. TOWNSEND,
Cashier.

Samuel V. Parsons was one of my owners; he lived in Buffalo. I mailed the check to him on the same day, Monday, October 11th. I was not in Oswego after that until along in December, I think. Mr. Parsons was there.

Question. Did you make any agreement with A. F. Smith & Co. to take this check absolutely as payment? Was anything said about it?

Answer. Nothing more than I have stated. It was conceded that this check was received by S. V. Parsons at Buffalo on the 13th of October, 1869, and was by him deposited in the Bank of Attica in
178   that city for collection; that on the same day it was mailed by the Bank of Attica to the Metropolitan National Bank of New York for collection; that on the 15th day of October, 1869, the check was presented at the Fourth National Bank of New York for payment, and payment was demanded and refused, and the same was protested for non-payment, and notice given to the endorsers.

On cross-examination by defendant's counsel, the witness testified: I was not informed while at Milwaukee that this wheat was for A. F. Smith & Co. by any one. When I arrived at Oswego I first tied up my vessel somewhere near the G. Ames elevator. There were two or three elevators between that and the Corn Exchange Elevator. I saw my vessel unloaded. No part of the wheat was spouted into a canal-boat to my knowledge. I think it was stored in the warehouse. Nothing was said by A. F. Smith & Co. to the effect that the wheat was for them.

On re-examination by plaintiffs' counsel, the witness testified: I had no interest in the schooner D. G. Fort nor in her freight I was simply master of the vessel.

It was conceded that Mr. Perry, the plaintiffs' attorney, re-
179   ceived this check from Samuel V. Parsons on or about the 17th or 18th of October, 1869, and that he at once went with it to the City Bank, and asked for payment of the freight, and the payment was refused. It was also conceded that a statement was made out by A. F.

Smith & Co., and signed by the master, Myron M. Holland, on the settlement of the freight as above stated. The statement was in the words and figures following, to wit:

OSWEGO, *October* 11, 1869.

Received per B. L. schooner Dan'l G. Fort, Holland, master, from Milwaukee Sept. 29, shipped by Mower, Church & Bell—

17,550 bus. 1 wheat, fr't 13c	$2,281 50
Less for 39.32/100 bus. sh't, $1.35	53 38
Shoveling	70 00
Elevating	43 78
P'd captain	2,114 34
	$2,281 50

Received payment as above.
(Signed)   M. M. HOLLAND.

There was an endorsement upon the back of said bill of lading in the words and figures following, to wit:

Received 17,550 bu., fr't 13c	$2,281 50
Less 39.32/100 bu. sh't, 1.35	53 38
Shoveling	70 00
180 Elevating	43 78
P'd captain	2,114 34
	$2,281 50

A. F. SMITH & CO.
F.

It was admitted that due diligence was used to collect the check given by A. F. Smith & Co. to Captain Holland.

It was admitted that the evidence of Forsyth, A. F. Smith, and Mannering was the same in this case as in that of Davison et al. vs. City Bank, and was used in the case of Parsons et al. vs. City Bank.

Said plaintiff also read in evidence from the testimony of A. F. Smith taken October 2d, 1872, in the cases against John Wilmot, as follows:

I have been engaged in the grain-elevator business since May, 1868, at Oswego. I am acquainted with the customs and usages of the grain-elevator business at Oswego, and I think generally throughout the West.

Q. Is it customary among these grain elevators to store in the elevators grain of the same grade received from different parties in separate and distinct bins?

181   A. I should say yes, except at the convenience of the elevator owners. If they had not sufficient room, of course they would put the same grades together.

The usage and custom is, in delivering grain from the elevator upon the orders, to deliver wheat of the grade called for from any bin containing that grade, to suit the convenience of the elevator when it would empty a bin.

When the elevators are busy and well filled, to convenience the elevator, it is our custom to mix grains of the same grade, knowing it to be of the same grade, although owned by different parties, and to deliver upon orders of the owners out of any and all bins in the elevator without any regard to the ownership of the grain as deposited.

The custom I have testified to is a general and, so far as I know, a universal custom among the grain elevators at Oswego and the West. The owners of the Corn Exchange elevator in 1869 were Delos De Wolf, president of the City Bank of Oswego, one-sixth part; Morris Winslow, president of the Merchants' Bank of Watertown, one-third; and I myself owned one-half.

Winslow bought his interest in the elevator about the fall of 1868.
182 De Wolf has owned his interest several years. A. F. Smith & Co. hired this elevator about the first of January, 1869, for one year, at an annual rent of about $5,000 or $6,000. A. F. Smith & Co. failed about October 16th, 1869. I presume we owed rent for the elevator at that time.

Whatever we owed has not been paid since. Our firm did not issue any warehouse or elevator receipts to any person or bank upon any of the grain received by us in September and October, 1869, from the schooners Atwater, D. G. Fort, Thomas Parsons, Garret Smith, Kate Kelly, Grenada, Corsican, and Atmosphere.

No person or bank ever applied to me or to our firm, to my knowledge, for any such receipts; neither myself nor my firm issued any receipt, vouchers, or other evidence of title to any part of the grain aforesaid received by us from any or all of said schooners so long as it remained in our elevator, and were never asked for any such papers by any person or bank so far as I know. The whole of the said grain was placed in our elevator, upon our elevator books, in the name, as owners, of A. F. Smith & Co. It was so entered at the time it was received, and remained so until its delivery.

183 Our firm of A. F. Smith & Co. obtained policies of insurance upon all the said wheat while in our elevator. All these policies were taken out in our own name. None of these policies were assigned, to my knowledge, to the Merchants' Bank of Watertown; nor was any interest in these policies invested in the Merchants' Bank.

When the aforesaid eight schooners arrived at Oswego their arrival was advertised in the Oswego public newspapers.

I had occasion to look in the custom-house at Oswego, and saw the captains' manifests of those eight cargoes of grain.

Between September 1st, 1869, and October 15th, 1869, we had in the elevator other grain than those eight cargoes.

184 And said plaintiff offered to read the following from the evidence of A. F. Smith, but to the reading of which defendant objected as irrelevant and incompetent, which objections the said judge sustained, and to which said ruling and exclusion of the evidence said plaintiff did then and there except. The testimony thus excluded is as follows:

I was well acquainted with Morris Winslow, president of Merchants' Bank, Watertown, and had known him a good many years—ten or twelve years. I was on intimate terms with him. I don't think he was in Oswego in the months of September and October, 1869. He usually stops at my house when he comes to Oswego. I think I did not visit Watertown several times in the months of September and October, 1869. I was there once, about the 12th day of October. Corresponded with the bank frequently. I mean A. F. Smith & Co. corresponded with the bank. Almost daily correspondence. We kept letter-press copies of letters addressed to them.

The exhibits hereto attached, marked, respectively, Exhibits 1, 2, 3, 4, 5, 6, 7, and 8, are copies of said correspondence.

185   A. F. Smith & Co. suspended payment on the 16th of October, 1869. I saw Morris Winslow, president of the Merchants' Bank of Watertown, two r three days after our suspension. I saw him at Oswego at our office first. He remained here a couple of days and stayed at my house while here. He may have gone back to Watertown the same night. He may have come here again. I cannot say how many times I saw him, but presume I saw Mr. Winslow several times while he was here. I was busy with the Milwaukee parties, Mr. George J. Jones and W. P. McLaren, and others who were on here at the time.

Q. At any of those interviews with Mr. Winslow, what, if anything, did he say relative to your shipment of the Milwaukee wheat to New York?

A. I do not claim to have had any interviews with him, and I had no conversation with him in regard to the wheat, to the best of my recollection. Winslow made no complaints of my conduct. The firm of Smith, Wemple & Co. was composed of the following members, viz: S. S. Smith, of Albany; V. Z. Wemple, of Albany; C. C. Risley, of Waterville, N. Y., and myself. Their place of business was 186   Albany. They were produce and commission merchants; dealt in hops, malt, flour, Western and Canada grain. That firm had existed five or six years, and I was a partner from the formation of the firm. There had been no change in the firm from its formation. I contributed capital to the firm: each member contributed $2,500. During the year 1869 A. F. Smith & Co., of Oswego, were in the habit of drawing drafts upon Smith, Wemple & Co. to large amounts. They were also in the habit of lending A. F. Smith & Co. considerable amounts in paper and money, for the accommodation of A. F. Smith & Co. A. F. Smith & Co. were in the habit of sending occasionally blank drafts on Smith, Wemple & Co. to the Merchants' Bank, Watertown, to be filled up as to date and time by the Merchants' Bank. The amount was always filled in. In one instance A. F. Smith & Co. authorized the Merchants' Bank by telegraph to draw a draft on Smith, Wemple & Co., sign our name to it, and place proceeds to our credit at their bank.

A. F. Smith & Co. drew sight drafts upon all the wheat shipped 187   by them from their elevator and consigned to David Dows & Co. and John Wilmot out of the cargoes of eight schooners above named. Our custom was to send these sight drafts, with bills of lading attached, to our correspondent banks in New York. These banks were the Fourth and Ninth National Banks of New York. I think all of these drafts went to these banks, and the proceeds placed to the credit of A. F. Smith & Co. The Merchants' Bank, Watertown, kept an account also with the said Ninth National Bank of New York.

188   Said A. F. Smith further testified, and which was read at the trial:

During the months of September and October I sometimes met with De Wolf and Mannering, but not in my elevator. I occasionally met them on the street, and, when I had business there, I met them in their bank. When I went to the bank, I went sometimes for financial business, sometimes for other purposes. I cannot say positively that I went to their bank in September or October, 1869, for financial purposes. I don't think I was at their bank in September or October, 1869, very often to obtain discounts. On the 23d of September, 1869, the City Bank discounted a draft drawn on Smith, Wemple & Co. for $5,000, for which A. F. Smith & Co. were credited $4,957.74, as appears by the books of A. F. Smith & Co. I believe the books to be correct. This is the only discount, except one of September 3rd, 1869, for $7,000, being a draft drawn on Smith, Wemple & Co. by A. F. Smith & Co., at fifteen days, which was discounted by City Bank, and A. F. Smith & Co. were credited $6,948.04. During September and October, 1869, our firm deposited with the City Bank sight drafts on New York several times. I presume I saw and talked to both De Wolf and Mannering during these months, but don't recollect.

Q. Did you hear any complaints from either De Wolf or Mannering during the months of September or October, 1869, as to your having shipped any of the Milwaukee grain referred to in these suits? If so, at what time did you first hear such complaints, and from whom?

A. I don't remember of ever hearing such complaints from either of them. My memory on this subject is clear, that I did not hear any such complaints before our failure; and if I have ever heard them say anything on the subject, it has been since our failure. They nor either of them have ever complained to me of my conduct for shipping said Milwaukee wheat to New York, & A. F. Smith & Co. used no concealment whatever in the shipment of any of the wheat in question in those suits in New York. The shipments were made in the ordinary way, and in the regular course of business; any one could have seen the shipments who chose to look. None of the grain of the eight lake vessels was mixed in the elevator.

Said plaintiff further read in evidence from the deposition of Sidney Bickford, taken by consent at Oswego, October 3rd, 1872, as follows, to wit:

SIDNEY BICKFORD, being duly called and sworn, testified as follows.

The cargo of the Kate Kelly was the first of the eight cargoes which arrived here. The Kate Kelly arrived September 16th, 1872; the Grenada arrived September 24th; Garret Smith arrived October 1st; Thomas Parsons, October 2d; the Atmosphere, October 3rd; Corsican, October 8th; the Atwater and D. G. Fort, October 9th. The first shipment of any of that grain to New York was made September 16th, by canal-boat Frank Alvord, consigned to John Wilmot, and the remainder of the said eight cargoes, that went to New York, were shipped as follows:

Sept. 18, per canal-boat Four Sisters, David Dows & Co.
"   27,   "   "   "   B. Hegeman,   "   "   "
Oct. 2,   "   "   "   Libbie Breed, John Wilmot.
"   2,   "   "   "   Enterprise,   "   "
"   4,   "   "   "   Norris Dennyman, David Dows & Co.
"   5,   "   "   "   Harman Post,   "   "   "
"   5,   "   "   "   E. D. Case,   "   "   "
"   8,   "   "   "   George Ames,   "   "   "
"   8,   "   "   "   Amie Rebecca,   "   "   "
Oct. 9, per canal-boat E. H. Shephard, John Wilmot.
Oct. 9, per canal-boat Mason Meloin, John Wilmot.
"   10,   "   "   "   P. B. Davis, Hughes, Hunt & Co.
Oct. 10, per canal-boat Alanson Post, Hughes, Holbrook & Co.

This is all of the said wheat that was consigned to New York.

The remainder of the said wheat was delivered by us as follows:

Sept. 16. A. C. Thomas, Mexico .... 360 bushels.
" 16. S. Graves & Co., Governor .... 310 "
" 16. Penthield & Stone .... 360 "
" 16. M. J. Cummings, Oswego .... 4,849$\frac{34}{60}$ "
" 18. J. F. Allen .... 100 "
" 25. Geo. Frazier & Co., Albany .... 360 "
" 25. Penfield, Lyon & Co., Oswego .... 2,000 "
" 25. David Salisbury, Woodville .... 200 "
" 25. M. J. Cummings .... 3,000 "
" 27. D. R. Hunebett, Orwell .... 100 "
" 27. J. C. Wright, Copenhagen .... 720 "
" 27. Poole & Clark .... 360 "
" 28. L. H. Mills, Stuknyville .... 662$\frac{9}{60}$ "
Oct. 1. Sylvester & Thompson, Mur .... 360 "
" 1. Shurl & Graves .... 640 "
" 1. A. Gilbert & Co., Centreville .... 360 "
" 1. Bryant Bros., Black River .... 300 "
" 1. C. E. Jones, Watertown .... 360 "
" 6. M. J. Cummings, Oswego .... 1,500 "
" 8. Mr. Merrick, Oswego .... 360 "
" 8. Jacob Amos, Syracuse .... 700 "
Oct. 8. L. Gill, Watertown .... 360 "
192 Oct. 11. A. C. Thomas, Mexico .... 360 bushels.
" 11. Sluyton & Stameson .... 360 "
Oct. 16. Lesfield & Shenlon, Herman .... 360 "
" 16. (Supposed) Randall & Kenyon, Adams (R. R.) 1,649$\frac{10}{60}$ "
" 16. (Supposed) Randall & Kenyon, Adams (R. R.) 124$\frac{42}{60}$ "
" 16. (Supposed) Randall & Kenyon, Adams (R. R.) 1,039$\frac{9}{60}$ "
" 16. Randall & Kenyon, Adams (R. R.) .... 600 "
" 16. (Supposed) Randall & Kenyon, Adams (R. R.) 1,013 "
" 16. " " " " " 95$\frac{28}{60}$ "
" 14. " " " " " 360 "

As to all that part of this wheat shipped to New York, A. F. Smith & Co. drew sight-drafts against it on consigners. The whole of these drafts, with the bills of lading annexed, were sent to either the Fourth or Ninth National Banks of New York, and the proceeds to be placed to the credit of A. F. Smith & Co. So far as I recollect, the proceeds of all those drafts were placed to the credit of A. F. Smith & Co., in one or the other of these banks. Besides these drafts on this wheat, other' were placed to our credit in these New York banks. There were 193 two instances in which those drafts on the wheat in question were placed to our credit in the First National Bank of Oswego.

The following drafts upon New York against said wheat were forwarded to the Ninth National Bank of New York, viz:

Sept. 16, 1869, for the sum of $9,490 00
Oct. 2, " " " " " " 8,510 00
" 4, " " " " " " 5,980 00
" 5, " " " " " " 8,426 00
" 8, " " " " " " 7,700 00
" 9, " " " " " " 8,405 00

REC. 473—5

There were forwarded of these drafts to the Fourth National Bank of New York the following, viz:

Sept. 18, 1869, for the sum of............................ $9,546 00
   27,   "   "   "   "   " 8,733 00
Oct. 2,   "   "   "   "   " 9,288 00
   8,   "   "   "   "   " 6,284 52

There were deposited to our credit in the First National Bank of Oswego, drafts as follows:

Oct. 5, 1869, for the sum of............................ $8,970 00
" 11,   "   "   "   "   " 8,415 00

We got our pay for all the wheat we sold out of said Milwaukee wheat to parties living in Watertown and vicinity by sending drafts to the Merchants' Bank, Watertown, and the proceeds to be placed to our credit in said bank. The following-named purchasers paid for 194 the price of the said wheat sold them out of this Milwaukee wheat, by paying our drafts at the Merchants' Bank, Watertown, viz: S. Graves & Co., J. C. Wright, Pool & Clark, L. H. Mills, Shead & Groves, L. Gill, Bryant Brothers, and C. E. Jones. These items amounted to about $4,500 to $5,000.

Q. Between the 15th day of September and the 16th day of October, 1869, how much moneys, standing to your credit in the Fourth and Ninth National Banks of New York, was paid by your firm to the Merchants' Bank of Watertown, by your checks in their favor upon said National Bank?

A. The following checks were sent by us to the Merchants' Bank of Watertown, upon the Fourth National Bank of New York, viz:

Sept. 17. Check for the sum of $1,232 24
   22.   "   "   "   "   " 8,000 00
   25.   "   "   "   "   " 10,325 00

The following certified check was sent by us to the Merchants' Bank of Watertown upon the Ninth National Bank of New York, viz:

Oct. 4, 1869, for the sum of............................ $11,000 00

195   Said plaintiff offered to read the following evidence from the said deposition of said Bickford, to wit:

In addition to these checks on the said Fourth and Ninth National Banks, we sent, between Sept. 15th and Oct. 16th, drafts on Smith, Wemple & Co., Albany, to the Merchants' Bank, to considerable amounts. Besides which the Merchants' Bank generally held our drafts on Smith, Wemple & Co., the amounts and signature filled in, but the dates and time left blank for them to fill up when they chose to place them to our credit.

The amounts of the said drafts on Smith, Wemple & Co., between Sept. 15th and Oct. 16th, 1869, placed to our credit in the Merchants' Bank were as follows:

Sept. 16. Draft on S., W. & Co. for sum of................ 10,000 00
   18.   "   "   "   "   "   " 5,000 00
   28.   "   "   "   "   "   " 9,000 00
Oct. 2.   "   "   "   "   "   " 5,000 00

These were all sight drafts. Our firm had heavy dealings with Smith, Wemple & Co. We were heavily indebted to that firm. On the first of October, 1869, it appears from our books that we were indebted to Smith, Wemple & Co. in the sum of $138,710.72. That debt arose wholly, 193 or nearly so, from their accommodation acceptances of our drafts to assist in our financial operations. When we stopped, on the 16th of October, 1869, we owed them in the same manner the sum of 70,761.22. We had reduced our indebtedness to this extent during those sixteen days, by $67,939.70, in the following way or manner:

Oct.	1. Draft on Ninth National Bank, remitted directly to them	$5,000 00
"	2. By draft on Ninth National Bank	10,000 00
"	7. " " " " " "	5,000 00
"	8. " " " " " "	5,000 00
"	10. By transfer of a debt due us from S. S. Smith, a partner of Smith, Wemple & Co.	10,015 00
"	13. Draft remitted	8,000 00
"	14. By Smith, Wemple & Co.'s acceptance, held by Hazer & Son, Watertown	20,000 00
	Returned by A. F. Smith by mortgage on elevator.	
"	14. By acceptance of Taylor, Albany, loaned us by Smith, Wemple & Co., and returned by us to them	10,173 25

Between the 16th of September and the 1st of October, Smith, Wemple & Co., received from us drafts on the Fourth and Ninth National Banks, New York:

Sept. 16.	Draft for	10,000 00
" 18.	" "	4,000 00
" 20.	" "	2,000 00
	Sept. 21. Draft for	3,000 00
197	Sept. 24. Draft for	2,800 00
	" 28. " "	4,000 00
Sept. 25.	Draft for	7,468 00

Our course of business was to procure from Smith, Wemple & Co., for our necessities, their accommodation acceptances, to be discounted, and to remit to them the funds to take up such acceptances at maturity. That was about all our business with them during the year 1869. Between the 16th of September and the 16th of October, 1869, the City Bank, Oswego, received from us the following drafts on the Fourth and Ninth National Banks of New York:

Sept. 17.	Draft on Fourth National B'k	$2,500 00
Oct. 4.	Checks on Ninth National B'k	5,100 00
Oct. 9.	There was deposited in the City Bank, for barley sold by us, to the amount of	12,675 00
" 14.	There was deposited by us in the City Bank	9,876 67

On October the 14th the Merchants' Bank charged to our account, and we gave them credit for it, $6,000, being our note held by that bank. This $6,000 note and another note of ours for $9,000, also held by that bank, had been held and carried by that bank by renewals for about two years previously. The $6,000 note was paid October 14th, as above 198 stated, and the $9,000 note was paid September 28th, 1869, by draft on Smith, Wemple & Co. According to our books, on the 1st day of October, 1869, we owed the Merchants' Bank, for overdrafts, $1,098.97, besides the $6,000 note above specified.

When we suspended payment on the 16th day of October, 1869, our account with the Merchants' Bank was   follows: As appears by our books, we owed them $549.02.

Besides the eight cargoes of Milwaukee wheat in question, A. F. Smith & Co. had no other wheat belonging to them between September 15th and October 16th, 1869, except about 63,000 bushels, bought by us in Toledo and Milwaukee about the same time of the wheat in question. This 63,000 bushels was bought some of it at sight and some of it upon short credit. It was all paid for before our failure. I rather think we had no other grain of our own in our elevator at that time. I saw Winslow when he came down here, after our failure. I had no particular conversation with him.

(Which offer was then and there objected to by said defendant as irrelevant and incompetent.

Objection sustained and evidence excluded, and to which said ruling and decision said plaintiff did then and there except.)

Said Bickford testified as follows:

199   A. F. Smith & Co. did business in and during the months of September and October, 1869, in barley, but do not recollect that we did in rye and oats. We have sold the barley on commission.

A. F. Smith & Co. also had transactions in wheat during such time other than the said eight cargoes in question. I don't think the firm of A. F. Smith & Co. made large advances on the barley that fall. I think the firm was not, during that time, indebted to Smith, Wemple & Co. for allowances made by them on barley at request of A. F. Smith & Co. When we (A. F. Smith & Co.) failed we were indebted to parties who owned the barley to the amount of about $8,000.

I have no recollection of the accommodation acceptances of Smith, Wemple & Co. being used in the barley transactions in the year 1869, and think they were not.

200   DELOS DE WOLF, recalled, testified that the defendant had money of the plaintiff, after the commencement of the suits to recover the freight, to the amount of $2,875.55. That money was received October 14th, by a check of A. F. Smith & Co. It was to pay the last draft due on the cargo of the Phalarope. That he refused to pay that money to the plaintiff while the freight cases were pending. That the defendant kept that money to indemnify it against judgments in those suits. That the defendant refused to give it up until it was settled what the judgments would be in the freight cases. The money stood to the credit of the plaintiff, and the *the* interest was credited to them, and Mr. French gave a check for it. I paid it to French February 21st, 1874. Amount paid, including interest, was $3,742.18. That included the interest. French was the attorney of the plaintiff. I suppose it went to pay the freight. I paid it to French. I refused to pay it until freight cases against defendant were settled. But for those cases, plaintiff would have been entitled to the $2,875 on the 14th day of October, 1869. Interest was paid from October 14, 1869, to Feb'y 21st, 1874.

201   ALBERTUS PERRY was called as a witness. It was admitted that he was an attorney and counsellor at law in the State of New York. And thereupon the plaintiffs offered to prove by said

witness what was a fair and reasonable compensation for the services of an attorney in the suit of the plaintiff against Hughes, Hickox & Co., in the circuit court of the United States in and for the southern district of New York, being an action of trover, where the recovery was 24,865 damages and costs $762.04 *costs,* and on which was collected $25,000. The evidence was objected   by counsel for defendant as irrelevant and incompetent. Objection sustained and evidence excluded, and to which said ruling and decision said defendant did then and there except.

Same offer as to value of services in the suit against John Wilmot, in which the recovery was 25,657 on damages, and nothing collected. Same objection, same ruling, and the evidence excluded; and to which said ruling said plaintiff did then and there except.

Said plaintiff did then and there offer to prove what the actual expenses were in such suits outside of att'y's fees, such as traveling expenses, &c. Same objection, the same ruling, the evidence excluded, and to which ruling and decision said plaintiff did then and there except.

202

GEORGE G. FRENCH was called and gave evidence tending to show that Woolworth was insolvent, and that he settled with him for the two thousand bushels of wheat, which he received by Maid of Judea, for $300.00, and gave him a full release therefor.

The defendant admitted that there was a break in the canal between Syracuse and Utica, by which the canal-boats were detained on the canal until the first of November, and that they did not arrive in New York until the fifth of November; that on that day the firm of Winslow and Vincott, att'ys of Hughes, Hickox & Co., notified the att'y of plaintiff of the arrival of the canal-boats to Hughes, Hickox & Co.

Mr. DeWolf testified that at one time he, A. F. Smith, and Thomas S. Mott were proprietors of the Corn Exchange elevator; Mott sold his interest to Smith; that he did not issue the card shown him; that he did not know of its issue until after it was withdrawn from the public; that he expected A. F. Smith issued it; that it was probably issued in 1868; when Smith came to Oswego; that he withdrew the card as soon as he heard of it, within a week after it was issued; Mott sold in 1868; Smith had no authority to issue the card; that he had been cashier of the def't bank from 1850 to 1865; that he said to Smith when he withdrew the card that we were not partners in running the elevator, and did not propose to be; that we could not allow him to run it in our name; Smith said it was inadvertently done, and was only to show the elevator was a responsible elevator.

203

The said card showed to the witness is as follows:

Corn Exchange Elevator,

Oswego, N. Y.

Capacity, 250,000 bushels.

4,000 bushels per hour.

5,000 barrels rolling freight.

Proprietors: Thos. S. Mott, Delos DeWolf, A. F. Smith.

Consignments promptly attended to.

The plaintiff further offered to prove the costs and expenses of conducting the freight cases, and to show what was a fair and reasonable

attorney's fees in conducting and carrying on the said suits to the court of appeals, which evidence was then and there objected to as irrelevant and incompetent by the counsel of the defendant. The objection
204   was sustained and the evidence excluded, and to which said ruling and decision said plaintiff did then and there except.

The said plaintiff thereupon rested. Said defendant offered in evidence and read an act of the legislature of the State of New York, passed April 18th, 1838, entitled "An act to authorize the business of banking," found in the laws of 1838, chapter 260.

Defendant's counsel read from the deposition of David Mannering, taken before A. B. Getty, as follows: I reside in Oswego; was cashier of the City Bank of Oswego in Sept. and October, 1869; Delos DeWolf was then and is now president of that bank; the bank received the letters and enclosures from T. L. Baker by due course of mail; the sight-drafts were paid, and time-drafts accepted by A. F. Smith & Co. The Atwater and D. G. Fort arrived with their cargoes at Oswego prior to maturity of time-drafts; the captains reported to me on arrival; I gave orders to captains to deliver their cargoes by writing orders on the captain's bills of lading. The receipts on the back of the bills of lading are in the handwriting of Mr. Forsyth, clerk of A. F. Smith & Co.
205   The Corn Exchange elevator is fitted up as an elevator and warehouse; have known it as such for ten years. A. F. Smith & Co. were its proprietors at the time I gave the orders to the captains; it was known in Oswego as a public warehouse and elevator. A. F. Smith & Co. were dealers in grain and commission merchants, and received grain for storage and transshipment as other elevators did; it was one of the largest in the city; it had storage capacity for 250,000 bushels; it is the only elevator in the city of that name. I redelivered to the captains the bills of lading after I wrote the orders on them. I obtained the bills of lading from Mr. Albertus Perry, for the purpose of producing them; they are not in my possession or under my control; the time drafts were not paid at maturity; and after their maturity I returned them and the bills of lading sent with them, to the plaintiff. I acknowledge the receipt of the letters, enclosing the drafts and bills of lading. Have resided in Oswego nineteen years and know it as a lake port at the mouth of Oswego River; I think the grain business is the largest business done in Oswego; it is done by commission merchants; most of the commission merchants are possessed of a
206   warehouse with an elevator; I think the number of warehouses with an elevator, in which commission merchants do their business in Oswego, is a peculiar feature of Oswego as a lake port. Oswego ranks first on Lake Ontario, and next to Buffalo, in reference to quantity of wheat received, on sale, on commission, or for shipment. The elevating warehouses at Oswego receive grain for storage merely. I should think there are 10 or 12 of these warehouses in Oswego; they all have some name; none of them are used exclusively for storing grain. A. F. Smith kept an account with defendant bank for two years. The Corn Exchange elevator was used by them and is such an elevator as I have described. The captains' bills of lading did not come from the plaintiff. They were brought to me by the captains. I did not see the captains' bills of lading until two weeks after I wrote the orders on them and gave them back to the captains; they were then in the captains' hands. I asked to look at them; they handed to me and I looked at them a moment and handed them back; since that time they have been in the custody of Mr. Perry. The receipts were then on the backs

207   of the bills of lading; the captains retained the bills with receipts endorsed thereon as their vouchers. I do not recollect whether I told the captains to collect their freight of A. F. Smith & Co. or not. I do not understand the letters of T. L. Baker to us instruct us to send the captains to A. F. Smith & Co. for the freight. The letter says A. F. Smith & Co. will pay all expenses. After the vessel was unladed I went over to the office of A. F. Smith & Co. for certificates of insurance of the property in store; they got the certificates and gave them to me; the bank did not pay for them; this was on the 9th of October, between five and six o'clock in the afternoon. The freight on the Atwater was 2,210; this might be reduced by charges for shortage; the bank did not ascertain whether any such charges were deducted; the plaintiff did not put defendant in funds to pay freight or other expenses. I do not know as it was our business to pay freight or expenses. We had received consignments by bill of lading from plaintiff, with drafts on A. F. Smith & Co., prior to the Atwater and D. G. Fort; we received some in July, 1869, in August, 1869, and in September, 1869. In those cases the sight drafts were paid and time drafts accepted before the arrival of the vessels. We acknowledge the receipts of the letters, and on the arrival of the vessels orders were given by us to captains to deliver cargoes to the Corn Exchange elevators; the next thing was to present the time drafts for payment; this was the course of business in all cases of receipts of bills of lading for account of plaintiff.

208

Q. In 1868 and 1869, did you receive consignments by bills of lading for account of any other bank in Milwaukee or other western banks, with drafts enclosed drawn on other commission houses at Oswego, than A. F. Smith & Co.?

A. Yes, sir, we did.

Q. In those cases, did or did not the wheat on arrival at Oswego go into the elevating warehouse or through the elevator of the parties on whom the drafts were drawn after acceptance of the drafts?

A. Yes, sir; it did when they had a warehouse.

Q. Was that the general usage at Oswego in cases of consignment by a bill of lading with drafts attached to banks at Oswego?

A. Yes, sir; I think it is and was at that time.

Q. Do you know whether the plaintiff, the Milwaukee National Bank of Wisconsin, had any knowledge or notice of that usage?

209   A. I don't know that they had any knowledge or notice.

Q. To what bank was this bank, the plaintiff, successor?

A. Their letter-heading received from that bank says they were successors to the State Bank of Wisconsin.

Q. Do you know how long the State Bank of Wisconsin and the bank which is plaintiff had been in the habit of making consignments by bill of lading to Oswego with drafts drawn against them?

A. No, sir; I don't know. I think we did receive such consignments from the State Bank of Wisconsin some years ago.

Q. How long has the usage prevailed in Oswego of ordering wheat on arrival at Oswego in the elevating warehouse of the merchant upon whom the drafts were drawn, if he had one?

A. I have no recollection of its being anything different since I can remember, some fifteen or sixteen years.

The exchange deducted by us was for placing funds in New York for the credit of the bank West. This was no more than the ordinary charge by the bank for collection and remittance. There was no charge for commission for looking after the property, nor any

210   agreement that we were to be paid for such services by the
plaintiff. The bank did not call for or receive warehouse receipts
for the cargoes of the Atwater or Fort. The transactions of A. F. Smith
& Co. in wheat before their failure had been large; down to the time of
their stoppage their credit in Oswego and with our bank was good. The
City Bank is situated in the city of Oswego; there is nothing between
the north window of the bank and the Corn Exchange Elevator to intercept the view of the elevator, unless it is vessels. I could see a vessel
and canal-boat at the Corn Exchange Elevator if there were no vessels
lying outside of the canal-boat, and could see the elevator working taking out the cargo from the vessel if the elevator was open so that I could
see the movement. Don't think I could see the whole of the Corn Exchange Elevator without putting my head outside of the window. I
could not tell whether the same grain that was passing out of the vessel
was going into a canal-boat; but could see that the leg of the elevator
211   was in one and the spout of the elevator was in the other. The
certificates of insurance were held to cover the cargoes of the Atwater and the Fort. On consignments to the bank from the West
the banks do not usually, according to the usual course of business, pay
the freights; it is paid by the party on whom the draft is drawn. I did
not see any of the cargoes of the Atwater or Fort in the elevator. I
first knew the wheat had been removed from the warehouse late on Saturday afternoon, October 16th, 1869. The reputation of A. F. Smith &
Co. as warehousemen in the city of Oswego at the date I signed the
orders on the captains' bills of lading of the Atwater and Fort was good;
they stood high as men of integrity. If we have warehouse receipts we
generally give them up when the drafts are paid. If they ask for an
order we give that when drafts are paid. No order is given on a bill of
lading when we have that. No order was given the warehousemen for
the delivery of these cargoes. When the drafts are paid we generally
deliver up the bills of lading and all the papers attached to the bill, except the letter received from the bank. If the drafts are protested, the
papers all go back to the bank from which we received them. From the
212   time we received these bills until returned to plaintiff they were
in our custody, except when drafts were sent over for acceptance.
It is our custom whenever we have any bills of lading to send
them over with the drafts and all papers that come with them, such as
the certificates of weight and inspection and insurance, and when accepted they are retained by our bank and kept by the bank, and when
drafts are paid they are given up if called for. The certificates of insurance and policies described the grain insured as in store. I paid no particular attention to the contents of the certificates. I did not look after
the cargoes after giving the orders to the captains.
Said defendant further read from the deposition of A. F. Smith, taken
at Oswego, on the
Said defendant read from the deposition of A. F. Smith, taken before
Judge Whitney, on the 17th day of February, 1870, as follows: " Our
house had no orders or permission from the plaintiff or City Bank of
Oswego to ship or dispose of these cargoes of wheat. I mean those of
213   the Atwater and D. G. Fort, and in the disposition of those cargoes we acted solely on our own responsibility. On the cargo of
the Atwater we attempted to pay the freight, as usual, and supposed we paid it. We gave our draft on New York to pay the freight.
It was not paid. Drafts were on Fourth National Bank, New York.
One draft was not paid, because there was an acceptance which we supposed another was to pay, which was charged by the bank to our account,

and left the balance too small to pay draft. We did not countermand the checks sent. Our account was good when we drew the checks.

Defendant read from the deposition of Sidney Bickford, taken before Judge Whitney Feb'y 17th, 1870, as follows: "The cargoes of the Atwater and Fort were disposed of in the way Smith has stated; they were disposed of for the benefit of our firm and by our firm; our firm had no permission or authority from the plaintiff or the City Bank of Oswego to make the disposition of these cargoes that we did that I know of.

It was conceded that the defendant held with the certificate of $5,000 obtained on the 9th of October, 1869, insurance upon grain in the elevator sufficient in amount to cover the drafts and acceptances of A. 214   F. Smith & Co. under the form of a policy, copy of which is attached to Mannering's deposition.

The form of that policy as to the description of the property insured is heretofore given in the bill of exceptions.

Counsel for defendant here states that they claim the draft of Taylor & Sons in the 4th National Bank; is not the same that defendant discounted, as the amounts are different.

The above and the foregoing is all of the evidence given on the trial of said cause.

And thereupon said defendant by its said counsel did then and there ask the said presiding judge to instruct the jury that the plaintiff had failed to make out a cause of action in its favor against the defendant, and to direct the jury to return a verdict for defendant: which motion said judge did then and there allow and grant, and to which said ruling and decision and the granting of the said motion said plaintiff did then and there except.

And said plaintiff by its said counsel did then and there insist that upon the evidence the plaintiff was entitled to recover, with in-215   terest, the amounts paid for freight on the cargoes of the Atwater and D. G. Fort, but the said presiding judge did then and there rule and decide that the plaintiff was not entitled to recover the said freight-money or any part of it, and to which said ruling and decision the plaintiff did then and there except.

And said plaintiff by its said counsel did then and there ask for leave to go to the jury on the question whether the defendant did not receive money the proceeds of the sales by Smith & Co. of the cargoes of the Atwater and D. G. Fort, and that the plaintiff was entitled to recover in this action from the defendant to the extent of the money which the evidence tends to show went into the hands of the defendant; but the said presiding judge did then and there rule and decide that the plaintiff could not go to the jury on that question, and to which said ruling and decision of said judge said plaintiff did then and there except.

And said plaintiff by its said counsel did then and there ask the said judge that the plaintiff might go to the jury upon the question whether, although the defendant pretends to say that it had no knowledge 216   of the shipment of the two cargoes by Smith & Co., that the defendant had in fact such notice, or in the exercise of reasonable care and prudence might have known of the shipments of the two cargoes that went to Hughes, Hickox, & Co., John Wilmot, and Woolworth, but the said presiding judge did then and there refuse and decline to grant said request, and to which said refusal said plaintiff by its said counsel did then and there except.

Said plaintiff further asked to go to the jury on the question whether the defendant exercised ordinary care and prudence such as a reasonable prudent person would exercise in selecting the warehouse known as the Corn Exchange Elevator of which A. F. Smith & Co., the person upon whom the drafts were drawn, were the proprietors; which said request the said presiding judge did then and there decline and refuse to grant, and to which said refusal said plaintiff did then and there except.

Said plaintiff by its said counsel did then and there ask the said presiding judge to allow said case to go to the jury upon the question whether Mr. Mannering, the cashier of the defendant, did not understand by our letters of instruction to him that A. F. Smith & Co. were to pay the freight as one of the conditions upon which they were to have the title to the property, which said request said presiding judge did then and there decline and refuse to give, and to which said refusal said plaintiff did then and there except.

Said plaintiff by its said counsel did then and there ask the said presiding judge to instruct the jury that as a matter of law the legal interpretation of the letters instruction sent by the plaintiff bank to the City Bank are that said bank was not to put the property either into the custody, control, or manuel possession of Smith & Co., until the payment of the draft drawn on these cargoes; which said request said presiding judge did then and there decline and refuse to give, and to which said refusal said plaintiff by its said counsel did then and there except.

And said plaintiff did further ask said presiding judge to instruct the jury that if they found from the evidence that the acceptance of Taylor & Sons was paid out of the funds of A. F. Smith & Co., derived from the sale of the wheat of the cargoes of the Atwater and Fort, that then and under such circumstances the plaintiff is entitled to recover in this suit the amount of the moneys thus received by the City Bank; which instruction said presiding judge did then and there refuse and decline to give, and to which said refusal to charge said plaintiff by his counsel did then and there except.

And said plaintiff further asked said presiding judge to instruct the jury that upon the undisputed facts in the case the plaintiff is entitled to recover all of the wheat which went to John Willmot up to the extent at least of the amount that is now due upon the unpaid time drafts; which said instruction said presiding judge did then and there refuse and decline to give to the jury, and to which said refusal said plaintiff did then and there except.

And thereupon the jury under the aforesaid charge of the said judge returned a verdict for the defendant and judgment in due form of law was entered on said verdict in favor of said defendant, and because said exceptions and none of them appear of record I have this thirteenth day of September, A. D. 1877, in pursuance of an order of said court made in said cause and at the request and with the consent of the respective parties, hereto set my hand and seal to this bill of exceptions.

Witness my hand and seal this thirteenth day of September, A. D. 1877.

HOYT H. WHEELER, [L. S.]
Judge.

220   (Indorsed:) U. S. circuit court, northern dist. N. Y. The Milwaukee National Bank of Wisconsin vs. The City Bank. (Copy.) Bill of exceptions. Filed Sep. 15, 1877.

221   In Supreme Court of the United States.

THE MILWAUKEE NATIONAL BANK OF WIS- ⎰
          cousin   ⎱
               vs.
     THE CITY BANK.

Know all men by these presents that we, The Milwaukee National Bank of Wisconsin, Charles T. Bradley, of Milwaukee, Wisconsin, and T. L. Baker, of the same place, are held and firmly bound unto The City Bank of the city of Oswego in the sum of two thousand dollars to be paid to the said The City Bank, its successors or assigns, to which payment well and truly to be made we bind ourselves and each of us jointly and severally, and our and each of our heirs, executors and administrators firmly by these presents, sealed with our seals and dated this first day of February, A. D. 1878.

Whereas the above named The Milwaukee National Bank of Wisconsin hath presented a writ of error to the Supreme Court of the United States to reverse the judgment rendered in the above entitled action by the circuit court of the United States in and for the northern district of New York:

222   Now therefore the condition of this obligation is such that if the above named The Milwaukee National Bank of Wisconsin shall prosecute its said writ of error to effect and answer all costs and damages if it shall fail to make good its plea, then this obligation shall be void, otherwise to remain in full force and virtue.

                    MILWAUKEE NATIONAL BANK OF WISCONSIN, [L. S.]
                              By CHAS. T. BRADLEY, *Pres.*
                              CHARLES T. BRADLEY.
                              T. L. BAKER.

In presence of—
     WILLIAM H. MORRIS.
     W. F. FILTER.

EASTERN DISTRICT OF WISCONSIN, *ss :*

Charles T. Bradley and T. L. Baker, the sureties above named, each for himself says that he is worth the sum of five thousand dollars over and above all debts, set-offs and exemptions, and further saith not.

                              CHARLES T. BRADLEY.
                              T. L. BAKER.

Subscribed & sworn to before me this 2d day of February, 1878.
[L. S.]   WILLIAM HENRY MORRIS,
                    Notary Public, Milwaukee County, Wisconsin.

223   EASTERN DISTRICT OF WISCONSIN, *ss :*

Be it remembered that on this 20th day of February, A. D. 1878, personally appeared before me the above-named Charles T. Bradley & T. L. Baker, known to me to be the persons who executed the above bond, and who acknowledged that they executed the same freely and voluntarily for the uses and purpose therein mentioned.

[L. S.]   WILLIAM H. MORRIS,
                    Notary Public, Milwaukee Co., Wisconsin.

I, Charles E. Dyer, of the district court of the United States for the eastern district of Wisconsin, do hereby certify that the within named obligors are known to me to be perfectly good and responsible for the sum of five thousand dollars.

CHAS. E. DYER,
U. S. District Judge, East'n Dist. Wisconsin.

224   (Indorsed:) Supreme Court U. S. The Milwaukee National Bank of Wisconsin vs. The City Bank. (Copy.) Bond. Within bond approved Feb'y 23, 1878. Wm. J. Wallace, U. S. dist. judge. Filed Feb'y 25, 1878.

225   UNITED STATES OF AMERICA, *ss:*

The President of the United States to the honorable the judge of the circuit court of the United States for the northern district of New York, greeting:

Because in the record and proceedings, as also in the rendition of the judgment of a plea which is in the said circuit court before you, between The Milwaukee National Bank of Wisconsin, plaintiff, and The City Bank, defendant, a manifest error hath happened, to the great damage of the said The Milwaukee National Bank of Wisconsin, as by its complaint appears: We being willing that error, if any hath been, should be duly corrected, and full and speedy justice done to the parties aforesaid in this behalf, do command you, if judgment be therein given, that then, under your seal, distinctly and openly, you send the record and proceedings aforesaid, with all things concerning the same, to the Supreme Court of the United States, together with this writ, so that you have the same at Washington on the second Monday of October next, in the said Supreme Court to be then and there held, that the record and proceedings aforesaid being inspected, the said Supreme Court may cause further to be done therein to correct that error, what of right, and according to the laws and customs of the United States, should be done.

Witness the honorable Morrison R. Waite, Chief Justice of the said Supreme Court, the 23d day of February, in the year of our Lord one thousand eight hundred and seventy-eight.

[SEAL.]   CHARLES MASON,
Clerk of the Circuit Court of the United States
for the Northern District of New York.

Allowed by—

WM. J. WALLACE,
U. S. Dist. Judge.

226   (Indorsed:) Supreme Court U. S. The Milwaukee Nat. Bank of Wisconsin, pl'ff in error, vs. The City Bank, def't in error. Writ of error. Filed Feb. 25, 1878.

227   The United States of America to The City Bank, greeting:

You are hereby cited and admonished to be and appear at a Supreme Court of the United States, to be holden at Washington on the second Monday of October next, pursuant to a writ of error filed in the clerk's office of the circuit court of the United States for the northern district of New York, wherein The Milwaukee National Bank of Wisconsin is plaintiff in error and you are defendant in error, to show cause, if any there be, why the judgment rendered against the said plaintiff in error as in the said writ of error mentioned should not be corrected, and why speedy justice should not be done to the parties in that behalf.

Witness the honorable William J. Wallace, judge of the circuit court of the United States for the northern district of New York, this twenty-third day of February, in the year of our Lord one thousand eight hundred and seventy-eight.

WM. J. WALLACE,
U. S. Dist. Judge.

228   (Indorsed:) U. S. Supreme Court. The Milwaukee National Bank of Wisconsin vs. The City Bank. Citation. Filed March 1, 1878.

I hereby admit due personal service on me of a copy of the within citation this 27th day of February, 1878.

ALBERTUS PERRY,
Attorney for the City Bank.

229   UNITED STATES OF AMERICA,
Northern District of New York, ss :

I, Charles Mason, clerk of the circuit court of the United States of America for the northern district of New York, do hereby certify that I have compared the writings annexed to this certificate, and they are true copies of their respective originals, and are correct transcript therefrom, now on file and remaining of record in my office, being a full and complete copy of the record and proceedings in the suit of The Milwaukee National Bank of Wisconsin vs. The City Bank.

In testimony whereof I have hereunto set my hand and duly affixed the seal of the said court, at the city of Utica, this 27th day of August, A. D. 1878.

[SEAL.]   CHARLES MASON, *Clerk.*

(Indorsed:) Supreme Court of the United States. The Milwaukee National Bank of Wisconsin, plaintiff in error, vs. The City Bank, defendant in error. Writ of error & return.

(Indorsement on cover:) No. 473. The Milwaukee National Bank of Wisconsin vs. The City Bank. N. New York C. C. U. S. Filed 11th September, 1878.

○

Supreme Court of the United States.

No. ~~178.~~ 198

THE MILWAUKEE NATIONAL BANK
OF WISCONSIN.

Plaintiff in Error,

against

THE CITY BANK,

Defendant in Error.

BRIEF.

H. M. FINCH,

Counsel for Plaintiff in Error.

In Supreme Court of the United States.

THE MILWAUKEE NATIONAL BANK,
OF WISCONSIN,

Plaintiff in Error,

vs.

THE CITY BANK,

Defendant in Error.

The plaintiff in error is a banking corporation in Milwaukee, Wisconsin. The defendant in error is a banking corporation in Oswego, New York.

The plaintiff, in its complaint, demands judgment against the defendant for sixty thousand dollars. The complaint alleges in substance, that on or about the 27th day of September, 1869, it discounted certain drafts for Mower, Church & Bell, of Milwaukee, and at the same time and in consideration of the discount, they—said Mower, Church & Bell—delivered to plaintiff bills of lading covering certain cargoes of wheat shipped by Mower, Church & Bell, from Milwaukee to Oswego, to be delivered at Oswego for account of T. L. Baker, cashier of plaintiff; that the defendant transmitted said drafts with the bills of lading to the defendant at Oswego *with specific instructions to hold the wheat for plaintiff until the drafts were paid, and that A. F. Smith & Co. would pay all expenses;* that the drafts, bills of lading and instructions were received in Oswego by the defendant; that for a good and valuable consideration the defendant undertook to collect the drafts and take charge of the wheat; that the vessels, with their cargoes, arrived in Oswego; that the defendant endorsed on the back of the bills of lading, *retained by the captains,* an order for the delivery of the cargoes, in these words: *"Deliver to the Corn Exchange Elevator for the account of T. L. Baker, Cashier, Milwaukee, subject to the order of the City Bank, Oswego, Oct. 9th 1869, D. Mannering, Cashier;"* that the cashier of defendant in and by said order did not make it a condition of the delivery of said cargoes that A. F. Smith & Co. should pay the freight; that said cashier well knew that said A. F. Smith & Co. were the proprietors of said elevator, and well knew that the wheat, under that order, would go into the possession of A. F. Smith & Co. before the payment of the drafts; that A. F. Smith & Co., upon the receipt of the wheat under said orders, sold and shipped the wheat, and received the money therefor, and paid the said money thus received to the defendant, who wrongfully applied the proceeds, and did not apply the proceeds to the payment of the drafts, but took and converted the money. It alleges that the shipment and sale by A. F. Smith & Co. was made with the knowledge, consent and approval of the defendant *and in violation of the instructions given by the plaintiff*. It also alleges non-payment of the freight on the cargoes of wheat, from Milwaukee to Oswego, and that the plaintiff was compelled to pay and did pay the freight. It also alleges the non-payment of the drafts, and *avers special damages and expenses of suits on account of the non-payment of the freight*, and that, by reason of the wrongful acts of the defendant, the plaintiff has sustained great damages, to-wit: to the amount of sixty thousand dollars.

The gist of the complaint is failure of the defendant *to obey the instructions of the plaintiff to hold the wheat until the drafts were paid and to collect all expenses of A. F. Smith & Co., a wrongful shipment of the wheat by A. F. Smith & Co., and a wrongful appropriation of the proceeds of the cargoes, and consequent loss by such wrongful acts to the plaintiff*.

The answer of the defendant is:—

1st. A general denial.

2nd. That A. F. Smith & Co., as proprietors of the Corn Exchange Elevator were warehousemen of good credit and repute, and engaged in the business of receiving grain for storage, and that defendants, as plaintiff well knew, had no place to store said wheat, and that the order given by said Mannering, Cashier of the defendant, was for storing said wheat for the plaintiff subject to the order of defendant.

3rd. That the defendant is a banking corporation, created under the laws of New York, and that the act of its Cashier in receiving and storing, or undertaking so to do, the said cargoes of wheat, was unauthorized and void.

4th. That plaintiff recovered, before the commencement of this suit, the value of said wheat, and has received thereby full satisfaction for the same.

The issue thus made came on for trial before the Honorable HOYT H. WHEELER, District Judge of Vermont, sitting as Circuit Judge at Canandaigua, in the Northern District of New York. Most of the facts were stipulated. After the evidence was all in the Judge, on request of the defendant, *directed the jury to return a verdict for the defendant*, and on this verdict judgment was entered in favor of the defendant.

The leading facts of the case are these: Messrs. Mower, Church & Bell, in September, 1869, were commission merchants in the City of Milwaukee. They received orders from A. F. Smith & Co., of Oswego to purchase two cargoes of wheat, and to draw therefor on A. F. Smith & Co. sight-drafts and also time-drafts against each cargo. In performance of these orders, Mower, Church & Bell purchased two cargoes of wheat in Milwaukee and shipped the same in two vessels called the Atwater and the D. G. Fort.

The cargo of the Atwater was 17,000 bushels of wheat. The cargo of the D. G. Fort was 17,500 bushels of wheat.

They drew drafts on A. F. Smith & Co. on the cargo of the Atwater as follows:

Draft dated on the 27th Sept., at 30 days......................$15,000.00
"   "   "   "   "   "   "   sight....................... 5,085.43
                                                                    _____
                                                                    $20,085.43

On the cargo of the D. G. Fort, as follows:

Draft, 29th Sept., at 30 days.................................$17,000.00
  "   "   "   "   . sight.................................. 4,052.62
                                                          _____
                                                           $21,052.62

Mower, Church & Bell presented the drafts and bills of lading to plaintiff who discounted the same. The bills of lading each recite that Mower, Church & Bell are the shippers, and by their terms make the cargo deliverable, at Oswego, to the account of T. L. Baker, Cashier of plaintiff, care of the City Bank.

The plaintiff, after discounting the drafts for Mower, Church & Bell, and receiving from them the bills of lading, enclosed the drafts and bills of lading to defendant's bank in the following letters:

MILWAUKEE, Sept. 29th, 1869.

D. MANNERING, Esq., Cash'r.

DEAR SIR: I enclose for collection and remittance to Nat. Park Bank, N. Y., bills as stated below. Your favor of   , with enclosure received:

A. F. Smith & Co., sight................................$5,085 43
  " "   "   "   30 Oct..............................15,000 00

B. L. schooner Atwater, 17,000 bushels wheat; in Ætna Ins. Co., 11,250; Home Insurance Co., 10,000; cer., weight and inspection. Please hold above certifs. insurance for arrival of vessel, *and on wheat going into store, please have it insured for enough to cover draft. On payment of the drafts you will please deliver the cargo to order of Messrs. Smith & Co. If not paid please hold and advise me by telegraph. Messrs. Smith & Co.* WILL PAY ALL EXPENSES.

Truly, Yours,

T. L. BAKER, Cash'r.

Also a letter dated Sept. 30, 1869, enclosing drafts, and also bills of lading of the D. G. Fort, in which is this language: "The instructions given you yesterday, and on all the cargoes shipped to you for Messrs. A. F. Smith & Co, you will please apply to this." The Cashier of the defendant acknowledged the receipt of the drafts and bills of lading by letters dated October 4th and 7th, and in the letter of the 4th says: *We prefer after this not to receive B. L. when we have to look after the property.* To this letter the cashier of the plaintiff replied as follows:

MILWAUKEE, Oct. 6th, 1869.

D. MANNERING, Esq., Cash'r.

DEAR SIR: I enclose for collection and   bills as stated below. Your favor of 4 with enclosures is received and note remarks.

We take very few time cargoes. *I would not take any unless we can hold the property. These cargoes were shipped to your bank at the request of Messrs. Smith & Co., and as you wrote me you charged extra for remitting, I suppose it was for the attention and care requisite.* The usual rate for remitting from Oswego is 1-10 c.; on this sight bill you have charged ¾. On 30th ult. I shipped you another cargo that I trust will receive your attention. I shall take no more time cargoes, and in the future will not ask you to look after the property on arrival.

Truly yours,

T. L. BAKER, Cas.

These letters of the plaintiff with the enclosures, were duly received by the defendant, and on the presentation of the drafts, A. F. Smith & Co., paid the sight drafts and accepted the time drafts. The defendant retained the bills of lading. A. F. Smith & Co. never obtained possession of the bills of lading.

The Atwater and D. G. Fort sailed from Milwaukee with the wheat on board, and arrived at Oswego on the evening of the 8th of October, and on the morning of the 9th of October the captains called upon D. Mannering, Cashier of the defendant, for an order for the delivery of their cargoes. The Cashier wrote on the back of each bill of lading *retained by the captains*, an order in these words: *"Deliver to the Corn Exchange Elevator for the account of T. L. Baker, Cashier, Milwaukee, subject to the order of the City Bank, Oswego, Oct. 9th, 1869, D. Mannering, Cashier"* (page 20). The Cashier testifies at folio 207, page 71, "I do not recollect whether I told the captains to collect their freight of A. F. Smith & Co. or not. I do not understand the letters of T. L. Baker to us, to send the captains to A. F. Smith & Co. for the freights. The letter says A. F. Smith & Co. "WILL PAY ALL EXPENSES." It will be observed that the order says nothing about the payment of freight. At folio 133, captain Davidson testifies that Mannering told him they—meaning the Corn Exchange Elevator—"would pay the freight." Captain Holland, at folio 176, testifies to the same fact, and at folio 211 Mannering testifies: "On consignments to the Bank from the West, the banks do not usually, according to the usual course of business, pay the freight; *it is paid by the party on whom the draft is drawn.*" On this evidence it is clear that Mannering should have understood the letter of instruction to mean that A. F. Smith & Co. were to pay the freight. Under this order the cargoes were delivered to the Corn Exchange Elevator. A. F. Smith & Co., the persons on whom the drafts were drawn, *were the sole proprietors of the Corn Exchange Elevator.*

No entry was made in the books of the Elevator that the wheat was received therein for the account of T. L. Baker, Cashier, Milwaukee subject to the order of the City Bank, Oswego, but it was entered *as the wheat of A. F. Smith & Co.* The defendant held no voucher of any kind, either from the captain of the vessels or A. F. Smith & Co., that the wheat had been delivered into the Corn Exchange Elevator or was stored there in pursuance of its order of delivery. At folio 161, the President testifies: "I made no inquiries after the order was given to the captains, and before the 16th, and I presume Mr. Mannering did not"; and at folio 171 he says: "By putting my head out of the window of this bank can see grain being discharged from the Elevator into the canal boat. I know they keep books in an Elevator. I never examined the books of the Elevator to see how A. F. Smith & Co. entered their cargoes. I suppose that under such an order as was given in these cases the cargoes would be entered as they were ordered to be. I did suppose that in this case, *under the order on the captain's bill of lading,* that Smith & Co. would enter the cargo on their books to the account of the Milwaukee Bank. *Of course I did not take the trouble to see how they entered it, because they run it off!!"*

The defendant thus allowed the wheat to pass into the possession of A. F. Smith & Co., not even taking a warehouse receipt, or any receipt or voucher on the bills of lading in their possession, or any writing of any kind, from anybody to show the disposition which had been made of the wheat. They made no inquiries in regard to it until it had been shipped out of the Elevator by A. F. Smith & Co., and was on its way to New York. Mr. Mannering, *after the vessels were unloaded*, went to the office of A. F. Smith & Co. for certificates of insurance, and obtaining them (folio 207). The form of the insurance certificate he received is given at folio 62. It does not purport to insure the wheat for plaintiff or the defendant, and it is a singular and yet undisputed fact that at the time the certificates were given the wheat *was not in fact in the elevator; the most of it had been shipped out of the elevator at the very time, and as fast as it was being placed in the Elevator!* The certificate was worthless in the hands of the defendant.

On the delivery of the cargoes at the Corn Exchange Elevator A. F. Smith & Co. made efforts to raise the money to pay the freight on the cargoes. Among other parties to whom they applied for money for that purpose was the defendant (folio 134, page 46). Being unable to raise the money to pay in full the freight, they finally settled with the captains by giving them some checks on the Oswego banks and checks or drafts on New York. Copies of the New York drafts are printed in full on page 35 of the printed case. These drafts were forwarded by the owners to New York city for collection and were not paid. The defendant was notified of their non-payment and refused to pay the freight, (folios 140, 141).

As we have already stated the captains of the Atwater and the D. G. Fort received their orders from the cashier of the defendant to deliver, on the 9th day of October, and on that day they proceeded to discharge the cargoes. On the same day the cargoes were discharged, there was purchased by Randall & Kenyon, from A. F. Smith & Co., of the cargo of the schooner Atwater, 7,700 bushels of wheat, and of the cargo of the D. G. Fort, 7,400 bushels, and by the directions of Randall & Kenyon, 7,700 bushels were, *on the same day* shipped into the canal boat A. Post, and 7,400 bushels into the canal boat P. B. Davis, and bills of lading were on that day signed by the captains of said boats, reciting that Randall & Kenyon were the shippers. They drew drafts on Hughes, Hickox & Co. of New York, against the shipments as follows: On the cargo of the Post $8,085.00, and on the cargo of the Davis $8,140. The drafts were paid by Hughes, Hickox & Co. The canal boats arrived in New York on the 5th day of November, 1869, and the wheat was delivered to Hughes, Hickox & Co., (folio 63 and 64).

On the same 9th day of October, A. F. Smith & Co. shipped out of the said cargoes as follows:

From the *Atwater* into Canal boat E. N. Shepard, to John Wilmot, New York, 7,641 26-60 bushels.

From the *D. G. Fort* into canal boat, Moses Melvin, to John Wilmot, New York, 7,650 bushels, and drew drafts on said shipments of $8,415.10, and $8,415. Wilmot paid these drafts. The wheat arrived in New York in November and was delivered to Wilmot.(folio 99, 100).

Immediately upon receipt of said wheat at said elevator, A. F. Smith & Co. entered the same in their books as for their own account. (folio 62) At the time they received said cargoes their reputation as warehousemen was good for honesty and integrity, and the warehouse had a storage capacity of 250,000 bushels, and was used for storing grain.

On the 18th day of October, *nine days after the wheat had been shipped* out of the warehouse, by A. F. Smith & Co., the defendant telegraphed plaintiff as follows: "*A. F. Smith & Co. have failed, you had better come here and look after your wheat!*" (folio 72).

The defendant knew on the afternoon of the 16th *that the wheat had been shipped,*(folio 160, page 55). To this telegraph plaintiff replied as follows: "*Do you hold wheat shipped to your care or delivered to consignee?*" And defendant replied back on the 19th: "*We stored the wheat for your account subject to our order, WE CAN NOT FIND IT.*"

We wish to call the attention of this Court to this telegram. It plainly shows that the defendants understood the duty they had to perform. It was, however, untrue that they had stored the wheat for the account of the plaintiff subject to their order. *It had not been stored at all.* The utmost they had done was to give an order for storage. But they did not know, and they had nothing in their possession to show that the wheat was stored. It had in fact been shipped without storage.

Mr. Hayden, the agent of the plaintiff, left Milwaukee on the evening of the 18th, and on his arrival in Oswego called upon the officers of the defendant. What took place at this interview is told by the President in these words: "I saw Mr. Hayden at the bank. He came to the bank and demanded the wheat, he said they should sue us for it. *I told him we stored it for their account and they ran it off, that I had no doubt they could find it,* that Smith had agreed to give the names of the boats it was shipped on. The conversation was short, the young man was quite set up, I thought, with his position, he was going to do something and I let him talk. *I told him I could not give him the wheat,* he was a young man. I told him I was willing to do anything I could for him, *and I had no doubt they would tell him where the wheat was!*" After the conversation Mr. Hayden seems to have tried to find where the wheat was, for on the 22d day of October he sent to Hughes, Hickox & Co., New York, the telegram, a copy of which is printed on page 25.

It appears by the record that it was agreed by the plaintiff, before any suit was commenced against Hughes, Hickox & Co., or John Wilmot, that the plaintiff would not replevy said wheat, but would sue in trover for the value thereof, and in consideration thereof, they, said Hughes, Hickox & Co., and said John Wilmot, would respectively, on the trial of such actions admit the receipt by them, respectively, of such wheat, (folio 126).

Suits in trover were afterwards commenced by plaintiff in the United States Circuit Court in the City of New York, against Hughes, Hickox & Co., and John Wilmot, for conversion of said wheat, and said defendant notified thereof. (See copy of notice page 34). This notice was dated on the 12th day of November, 1869. Judgments were recovered in each of said suits for the full value of the wheat alleged to have been received by them. (folio 123). During the progress of said trover suits the two notices on page 36 and 37, were served by plaintiff upon the defendants.

It is also stipulated that 2,005 bushels of the wheat was shipped to one Woolworth, and he, being insolvent, plaintiff settled with him for $300, that Randall & Kenyon purchased all the balance of said cargoes, and that plaintiff settled with them for said balance by receiving $2,473.73 in full of said balance; that Hughes, Hickox & Co. paid $25,657.04 to plaintiff in satisfaction of the judgment against them, (folio 123). *Aside from these payments no part of the time drafts have been paid.* Evidence was also given tending to show, and showing, that it was the custom in Oswego to deliver wheat into the warehouses of the acceptors of drafts when such acceptors were proprietors of a warehouse, *and to have it stored for the holder of the drafts subject to the order of the bank holding the drafts,* (folio 165).

There is evidence tending to show that A. F. Smith & Co. did a large loan and discount business with the defendant bank. A copy of the debt and credit of the account on the Ledger of the Bank will be found on pages 39 and 40. It will be seen that from August 2d, 1869, to October 25th the debits were $178,226.45, And it will be observed that on the credit side there was paid to defendants' in checks from October 4th to the 14th; *a period of ten days,* the large sum of $20,651.67.

It appears from the evidence that A. F. Smith & Co. must have pre-determined a great fraud. They ordered to be purchased eight cargoes of wheat in Milwaukee, *on credit,* (folio 190). They requested the drafts on these two cargoes to be sent to defendant. This vast quantity of wheat on its arrival was ordered by the banks to whose care it was consigned to be delivered to the Corn Exchange Elevator by orders worded the same as the orders in this suit, and on the very days the wheat was received at the Elevator, most of it was shipped out of the elevator by A. F. Smith & Co. Large quantities of the wheat was sent to various parties in New York. Sight drafts were drawn on these New York parties, and paid. (The case of Dows vs. Bank, 1st Otto 618, arose out of these shipments).

These drafts were all paid in good faith by the New York parties. The wheat not sent to New York was sold to millers and other parties in various quantities, and in various places, and the cash received therefor, (folio 190 to 193). The proceeds of the drafts on the New York parties were placed either in the 4th or 9th National Banks in New York City, to the credit of A. F. Smith & Co., *and A. F. Smith & Co. gave to defendants some checks on the 9th National Bank.* At folio 162 will be found the vague, unsatisfactory testimony of the President of the defendant as to the receipt of checks from A. F. Smith & Co., covering the large amount of money, aggregating $20,651.67, of which sum $12,675 was received on *the very day the plaintiff's wheat was shipped out of the Corn Exchange Elevator.* A. F. Smith, at folio 189, testifies: "That during September *and October,* 1869, our firm deposited with the City Bank (the defendants) *sight drafts on New York several times,*" and at folio 154 the President of defendant testifies that A. F. Smith & Co., borrowed money of defendant "on their own notes *and on drafts on New York.*"

It is also evident from the testimony of Sidney Bickford, of the firm of A. F. Smith & Co., on pages 64 to 68, that the money paid to the defendants, after the 9th of October, if not that paid on the 9th, was the proceeds of the cargoes of the Atwater and D. G. Fort. They had sold and shipped the entire eight cargoes. The drafts they drew on New York against the cargoes of the Atwater and D. G. Fort alone aggregated a little over $33,000, and there was in addition the money realized from the sale of the 2,000 bushels to Woolworth, and the amount paid by Randall & Kenyon for the balance of the cargoes. They had shipped all of the other cargoes prior to the 9th of October, (see statement of shipments, page 64) and had deposited the proceeds of the drafts on New York, in the 9th and 4th National Banks of New York and the First National Bank of Oswego. They had paid Smith, Wemple & Co, between the 1st day of October, 1869, and the 16th day of October, 1869, $67,939.70. They had also paid a large indebtedness to the Merchant's Bank and all of the sight drafts on the cargoes. And it appears from the ledger statement of the defendant (page 39) that on the *9th day of October* A. F. Smith & Co. drew out of the defendant bank $11,500.00, and on the same day (page 40) deposited $12,675.00, and yet, when on the afternoon of that day Bickford, of A. F. Smith & Co., applied to defendant for money to pay the freight on the cargoes of the Atwater and D. G. Fort *the defendant refused his request!*

The captain of the Atwater testifies (folio 134) that his vessel was unloaded "in the vicinity of four o'clock in the afternoon." He then details the attempt to get his freight money of A. F. Smith & Co., and says, on page 46: "Mr. Bickford stated that he had been unable to raise any money, that he had been to several banks, among the rest of the banks he *had been to the City Bank and he could not get any money.*" This is an important fact and it is not denied by any officer of the defendant. The President and Cashier were both called as witnesses, and neither denies this fact.

It is not perceived why this request should not have been granted. The sight drafts on the cargoes had been paid, and if the wheat was actually stored in the warehouse, as directed, the wheat was there to reimburse the defendant for its advance. The refusal is evidence that the defendant was afraid to trust A. F. Smith & Co. with the wheat for the purpose of securing payment of the small amount due on it for freight.

The record shows that the drafts on New York given to the captains towards payment of the freight were duly presented for payment and payment refused. The owners of the vessels brought suit against defendant for the freight.

The defendant notified the plaintiff of the bringing of the said suits, and tendered the defence thereof to the plaintiff. The plaintiff thereupon gave the defendant the notice published on page 35. Shortly after these suits were commenced the defendant received from other sources than the cargoes of the Atwater and Fort, money of the plaintiff to the amount of *$2,875.55* proceeds of certain drafts it had collected for plaintiff.

This money the defendant *refused to pay to plaintiff until the suits to recover the freight were determined.* (folio 200)

The suits to recover the freight were tried in the Supreme Court of New York, and judgment went against the defendant. The defendant still refusing to pay over the $2,875.55 it had collected and retained, the plaintiff furnished sureties upon bonds to pay the judgments in case the judgments were affirmed on appeal and appealed the case to the New York Court of Appeals. The judgments were affirmed. (See 57th N. Y. Reports, page 85 for the opinion). After the judgments were affirmed, and in order to protect its bondsmen as well as obtain its $2,875.55 withheld by defendant, plaintiff paid the judgments. And afterwards the defendant paid the plaintiff the said $2,875.55 with interest making the total paid $3,742.18.

The plaintiff in order to indemnify and save harmless, its sureties was obliged to pay and did pay $4,477.83, the amount of such judgments of which payment it notified the defendant Bank by the notice, a copy of which is printed on page 38, and demanded the amount of the defendant.

The defendant has never paid to plaintiff this amount or the expenses of the said suits.

The plaintiff specially alleges as part of its damages the expenses attending these suits and offered to prove the same, but the offer was rejected and plaintiff excepted. (See pages 69 and top of page 70).

The plaintiff offered to prove the fair and reasonable compensation of counsel for services in the trover suits against Hickox & Co. and John Wilmot, also its actual expenses, outside of attorneys fees, in and about said suits, but the offer was rejected and plaintiff duly excepted, (folio 291).

It is believed that the foregoing statement of facts is accurate, and full enough to present the main points involved on this writ of error.

ASSIGNMENT OF ERRORS.

1st. The Court erred in taking the case from the jury and instructing them to find for the defendant.

2d. The court erred in refusing to charge the jury that the plaintiff was entitled to recover with interest the amount paid for freight due on the cargoes of the Atwater and Fort, (folio 215.)

3rd. The Court erred in ruling and deciding that plaintiff could not, upon the proofs, recover the amount paid for freight money.

4th. In not allowing the plaintiff to go to the jury on the question whether the defendant did not receive and appropriate to its own use money, the proceeds of the cargoes of the Atwater and Fort, (folio 215).

5th. In not charging, as requested, that if the defendant did receive said money, said plaintiff was entitled to recover it in this action, (folio 215).

6th. In not allowing the jury to find whether defendant did not have notice, or in the exercise of reasonably care might have had notice of the shipment of portions of the two cargoes to Hughes, Hickcox & Co., and John Wilmot.

7th. In not allowing the jury to find whether the defendant exercised ordinary care and prudence in selecting the warehouse of which A. F. Smith & Co., were the proprietors, as the warehouse to store the wheat, and in not seeing that the wheat was stored in the Corn Exchange Elevator in pursuance of the terms of the order of delivery written on the captains' bills of lading.

8th. In not allowing the jury to find whether the Cashier of the defendant did not understand the letter of instructions to him, to mean that A. F. Smith & Co., were to pay the freight, as one of the conditions of delivering the wheat to A. F. Smith & Co., (folio 217).

9th. In refusing to charge the jury that the letters of instruction of plaintiff to the defendant in their legal effort were that the wheat was not to go into the custody, control and manual possession of A. F. Smith & Co., until payment of the drafts, and the freight.

10th. To the refusal of the judge to allow the jury to find from the evidence whether the acceptance of Taylor & Sons, credited in the ledger account of the defendant under date of September 24th, and due October 16th, was paid out of the sales of the wheat from the schooners Atwater and D. G Fort.

11th. The refusal of the judge to charge that if the said Taylor draft was thus paid, the plaintiff was entitled to recover the amount thereof.

13th. The refusal of the judge to charge the jury that upon the undisputed facts of this case, the plaintiff was entitled to recover the value of all of the wheat which came from the cargoes of the Atwater and Fort, and went into the hands of John Wilmot at least to the extent of the amount due on the unpaid drafts.

14th. In refusing to allow the plaintiff to prove the costs and expenses of the trover suits against Hughes, Hickcox & Co., and John Wilmot, the expenses in hunting up the wheat, and the costs and expenses of the freight suits.

ARGUMENT.

I.

The rule of law which is to govern the presiding judge, in a jury trial, in taking a case from the jury, is well stated in the opinion of Justice MILLER in the case of *Pleasants vs. Fants*, 22d Wallace 122. "Conceding", he says, "all the inferences which the jury could justifiable draw from the testimony if the evidence is insufficient to warrant a verdict for the plaintiff, the court should say so to the jury." Or, as chief Justice MARSHALL said, in *Bank of Washington vs. Triplet & Neale*, 1st Peters 31,—"The first prayer of the defendant in the Circuit Court, being to instruct the jury, that, upon the whole evidence, the plaintiff ought not to recover, if it might properly have been granted, in any case, in which any testimony was offered, *certainly ought not to have been granted, if any possible construction of that testimony would have supported the action*." Or, as is said in *Battles et al. vs. Landensluger*, 84th Pa. State, Rep., 452,—"If there is evidence on which the jury can properly find the question for the party on whom the onus of proof lies it should be submitted, if not it should be withdrawn from the jury."

Now in this case the plaintiff in error not only claims that this record contains evidence from which the jury "could properly find for the plaintiff," but it insists that *a verdict of a jury against the plaintiff would have been plainly and palpably against the evidence*. Indeed the evidence seems to be so strong and conclusive against the defendant that the plaintiff might well have been entitled to an affirmative direction from the court, that a right of action existed in favor of the plaintiff against the defendant.

In order then to establish that there was and is sufficient evidence in this case upon which the jury "could properly find" for the plaintiff, we propose to consider the facts in several different aspects.

1st. There is evidence in the case from which the jury "could properly find" that there was actual fraud and collusion between A. F. Smith & Co., and the defendant, to so place the two cargoes of wheat into the possession of A. F. Smith & Co., as to enable them to make an immediate shipment of the wheat for their own account and without payment of the time drafts.

2d. There is evidence in the case from which the jury might "properly and legally find" that the defendant did not exercise ordinary care and prudence in the transaction of the business, and that in consequence of such want of care and prudence the plaintiffs were greatly damaged.

3d. The undisputed evidence is that A. F. Smith & Co. were selected by the defendant as its agent, to receive and store the wheat for the account of T. L. Baker, the Cashier of the plaintiff, subject to the order of the defendant, *and that A. F. Smith & Co., immediately on receiving the wheat, without storing the wheat at all, shipped it to New York, and other places, and received the proceeds, and did not pay the time drafts or freight.*

4th. There is evidence in this case from which the jury "could properly find" that the defendant by the exercise of ordinary care, could have learned of said shipments being made in time to have prevented them.

5th. There is evidence from which the jury "could properly find" that the letters of instruction of plaintiff to defendant were knowingly or at least negligently violated.

6th. There is evidence from which the jury "could properly find" that the Cashier of the defendant well knew and understood that the language in the letter of instructions, "*A. F. Smith & Co. will pay all expenses,*" included the payment of freight on the cargoes from Milwaukee to Oswego.

7th. There is evidence from which the jury might and "could properly find" that by reason of the neglect of the defendant in not making payment of the freight by A. F. Smith & Co., a condition of the delivery of the cargoes, the plaintiff sustained damages to the amount of the freight unpaid by A. F. Smith & Co.

8th. There is evidence in the case from which the jury "might properly find" that the wheat, on its delivery at the Elevator, was entered on the books of the Elevator as the wheat of A. F. Smith & Co.; that no warehouse receipt was taken from A. F. Smith & Co. by the defendant, and no voucher or writing of any kind from any person was received or held by the defendant to show that the order of delivery was complied with by an actual storage of the wheat, in the Corn Exchange Elevator, for the account of T. L. Baker, cashier, subject to the order of the City Bank; and that no officer of the bank took any steps whatever to know that the order of delivery had been complied with.

9th. There is evidence in the case showing that the telegram of the defendants dated on the 19th of October, (folio 73,) "*We stored this wheat for your account subject to our order. We cannot find it,*" was untrue in that the wheat was never stored in the Corn Exchange Elevator at all, to the order of anyone. It was mostly "spouted" directly from the vessels through the elevator into canal boats, and had been shipped out of the elevator several days before the telegram was sent.

10th. There is evidence to show that Bickford, of the firm of A. F.

Smith & Co., applied to defendant for money to pay the freight on the cargoes of the Atwater and Fort, and the defendant refused his request.

II.

The evidence discloses clearly enough that Mower, Church & Bell were the original purchasers of the wheat in Milwaukee; that they purchased the wheat on the order of A. F. Smith & Co., and drew drafts on A. F. Smith & Co. to reimburse themselves for the money paid for the wheat; that they received from the captains of the Atwater and D. G. Fort bills of lading reciting that they were the shippers, and making the wheat deliverable in Oswego for account of the cashier of the plaintiff, care of the City Bank; that they presented the bills of lading with the drafts to the plaintiff; that plaintiff discounted the drafts, received the bills of lading, and transmitted the drafts and bills of lading to defendant *with explicit instructions to hold the wheat until payment of the drafts, and that A. F. Smith & Co. would pay all expenses.*

It must be conceded that under these circumstances the title to the wheat was in the plaintiff and it had the right to impose such conditions as it pleased upon A. F. Smith & Co. as to vesting them with the title, and that A. F. Smith & Co. could not obtain the title until the conditions were complied with. [*Dows vs. National Exchange Bank of Milwaukee*, 1st Otto 618.]

It must be further conceded that the plaintiff did not lose its title to the wheat by the acts of the defendant, and that the shipment of the wheat by A. F. Smith & Co. was a wrongful and tortious act and gave no title as against the plaintiff to the vendees of A. F. Smith & Co., although they purchased in good faith and without notice of the rights of the plaintiff. [*Dows vs. National Exchange Bank*, 1st Otto, 618, and *Heiskell vs. F. & M. National Bank*, 89th Pa. State Rep., 155.]

But while thus conceding that the legal title to the wheat was as fully in the plaintiff after its shipment by A. F. Smith & Co., as it was before the order of delivery was given by the cashier of the defendant, and while conceding that the defendant was utterly powerless to pass the legal title of the wheat to any party until the conditions imposed by the plaintiff were complied with, I do not, therefore, or thereby concede that the plaintiff has no legal cause of action against the defendant to recover damages for the wrongful acts, neglects and defaults of defendant and its agents in receiving, caring for, or selling the wheat. The damages of the plaintiff are *prima facie* the value of the wheat with interest, and all reasonable costs and expenses necessarily incident to and proximately connected with those wrongful acts, neglects and defaults. Nor does the fact that the plaintiff might or could institute legal proceedings against any and all third parties who had purchased the wheat in good faith from A. F. Smith & Co., and thereby could recover the wheat or its value from such third parties, impair or destroy *the right of action* of plaintiff against defendant for the wrongful acts, neglects or defaults of defendant and its agents.

On the contrary, I assert and maintain that notwithstanding the plaintiff has not lost, and could not lose, by the wrongful acts or defaults of defendant, the legal title to the wheat, and notwithstanding that defendant was powerless to vest any third party with the title to the wheat until all the conditions imposed by plaintiff were fully performed, and notwithstanding the plaintiff has a valid cause of action against A. F. Smith & Co. and any and all persons purchasing or receiving the wheat of the plaintiff from A. F. Smith & Co., and might and could, by proper legal proceedings, recover of and from all such third parties, the wheat thus received, or its value. Until plaintiff has *actually recovered the wheat, or its value,* it has a valid cause of action against defendant for all the damage it has sustained by reason or on account of the wrongs, neglects or defaults of defendant or its agents.

Nay, more, I assert and maintain that if it had appeared on the trial of this cause that the plaintiff then had obtained from such third parties, with or without suit, the wheat, or its value, that even then the plaintiff would have a *legal right of action* against defendant for its wrongful acts or defaults, and the fact that plaintiff had obtained the possession of the wheat or received its value, would only mitigate the damages. The possession of the wheat, or the receipt of its value would not, of itself, impair or destroy *the right of action.* It would of course mitigate the damages. But *the right of action* would remain intact, complete and perfect in the plaintiff to recover any and all expenses beyond the value of the wheat which were reasonable, necessary and proper to incur, and were actually incurred, to obtain the wheat or its value, and all damages which were and might legally be the necessary and proximate result of the acts, neglects or defaults of defendant or its agents.

The distinction between a right of action still existing, and the measure of damages in the action, in case any evidence is given to mitigate the damages, should be kept in mind. While the damages might be mitigated the right of action would still remain valid.

I claim that although the legal title of the wheat is valid in the plaintiff as against innocent third parties, and although the plaintiff may have a good cause of action against those claiming to hold, and holding the wheat, yet until the plaintiff has actually become possessed of the wheat, or its value, the damages the plaintiff has sustained by the wrongful acts or defaults of the defendant is the value of the wheat and interest to the extent of the unpaid drafts, and all expenses necessarily and reasonably incurred by plaintiff occasioned by or proximately resulting from such wrongful acts or defaults.

In *Murray vs. Burling,* 10th Johns, 172, the plaintiff brought an action of trover for the conversion of a promissory note. *The plaintiff had possession of the note at the time of the trial.* The Court, on motion of the defendant, granted a non-suit. Writ of Error was sued out and the judgment reversed.

THOMPSON, J., on page 176, says:—"That the plaintiffs have paid up their note, and have it now in their possession, is no objection to maintaining trover for the damages sustained by the conversion. It is every day's practice to sustain this action for the injury suffered, *although the owner has re-possessed himself of his property* (2 *Esp. N. P.,* 190, 191). *The note went into the defendant's hands as the plaintiff's property, and it is the misuse, or disposition of it,* CONTRARY TO ORDERS, *that constitutes the cause of action.* It is no answer to say that the plaintiff has a remedy by an action for the money. There are many cases in which a party has an election of actions. As if I entrust a man with my horse to ride and he sells him, I may bring trover against him for the horse, or affirm the sale and bring an action for the money. The defendant comes with an ill grace to turn the plaintiff round to another form of action which may better accommodate his own views. It is a sound maxim that no man shall found any claim or defense upon his own iniquity. There cannot be a doubt but that the defendant is liable in some form of action, and we see no objection to maintaining trover."

In the case at bar the plaintiff did not recover all of its wheat, or its value, and the time drafts are not all paid. But had the plaintiff recovered enough wheat or its value to pay the unpaid time drafts and interest, yet the facts in the record show actual damage sustained beyond the unpaid time drafts. The plaintiff was still damaged to the extent of the freight unpaid by A. F. Smith & Co., and all of its necessary costs and expenses in looking up the wheat, and all the costs and expenses of the trover suits and the freight suits. To the extent of some or all of these expenses the plaintiff, even if it had recovered the wheat or received its value to the extent of the unpaid time drafts, had a good cause of action against the defendant. To the extent that the plaintiff has recovered the wheat or its value the damages are without doubt mitigated. But it is not perceived how the mere fact that the plaintiff did not and could not lose the legal title to the wheat in the possession of third parties by the wrongful acts or defaults of the defendant could have greater or even as much efficacy to impair or destroy the right of action of plaintiff against defendant, as the actual possession of the wheat, or the actual receipt of its value before or at the trial. If the actual possession of the wheat, or the actual receipt of its value, by the plaintiff, at or before the trial, would not necessarily defeat the plaintiff's right of action, then it would seem to follow very clearly, that, although the legal title of the wheat was good in the plaintiff, even against innocent third parties, notwithstanding the tort of the defendant, and in spite of that tort, a valid cause of action would still exist in favor of the plaintiff against the defendant, for the wrongful acts, neglects, and defaults of defendant and its agents. And I insist that as there is no evidence in this record showing that the plaintiff has obtained possession of enough of its wheat, or received the value of enough of it, to pay all of its time drafts, that to the extent of the unpaid time drafts, the unpaid freight money, and all the necessary costs, charges, and expenses of looking after the wheat, the expenses of the trover suits, and the costs and expenses of the freight suits, are still subsisting and legal damages which plaintiff is entitled to recover of and from defendant, and which were occasioned and suffered by the wrongful acts, neglects, and defaults of defendant and its agents. In other words, what I mean is, that if the wheat of the plaintiff, by the wrongful acts, neglects, or defaults of the defendant is found by the plaintiff to be in the possession of third, parties claiming title to it in good faith, by purchase from A. F. Smith & Co., and such parties refuse to surrender to plaintiff the wheat thus purchased, or to pay its value, although the plaintiff might and could successfully maintain replevin for the wheat, that such fact does not, cannot, and will not operate to defeat the plaintiff's right of action against defendant for the wrongful acts, neglects, or defaults of defendant or its agent. Such a legal right of action does not operate, *per se*, to mitigate the damages, much less does it operate to abate or to bar the action of the plaintiff. And it certainly is not as powerful to abate or to bar the action of plaintiff as the actual receipt of the value of the wheat, or the actual possession of the wheat.

The authorities are full to the point that the mere fact that the owner of personal property has succeeded before the trial in recovering actual possession of the property, will not, of itself, defeat an action of trover to recover damages for the conversion of the property. It will not be necessary to cite but two or three additional cases to show how well sustained is this proposition.

But as already stated, the defendant has not shown that plaintiff has recovered possession of enough wheat to pay its unpaid time drafts. All that defendant has shown is that plaintiff has a right of action or claim against third parties claiming title in good faith by purchase from A. F. Smith & Co. This is certainly not the equivalent of possession or the actual receipt of value.

In *Ford vs. Williams*, 24th N. Y., 366, it is said: "It is no defense to an action of trover or trespass that the plaintiff *has got back his property which the defendant wrongfully took or converted. In such case the measure of damages is the sum paid to obtain the property.*"

In *McDermott vs. North*, 47th Barb., 530, it was claimed that the justice erred in allowing evidence as to what it was worth per day to look for the lost hogs in question. The Court say: "The general rule as to the measure of damages in an action of trover undoubtedly is the value of the property detained, with interest. But the rule has many exceptions, and among them is the case where the plaintiff, being the true owner, *has been subjected to the loss of time or the payment of money in searching for the property unlawfully taken, in which case a reasonable allowance may be made by the jury for such time and expense in addition to the value of the property and interest.*"

The case of *Bennett vs. Lockwood*, 20th Wendell, 224, lays down the same rule. In this case NELSON, C. J., says: "The defendant took the horse and wagon of the plaintiffs wrongfully, and used them, by reason of which taking the plaintiffs were induced to believe that the person to whom they had hired it temporarily had absconded, and therefore *they went in pursuit of their property and expended time and money * * * Here the damages were duly claimed:—they occurred in the use of reasonable means on the part of the plaintiffs to re-possess themselves of their property, and were occasioned by the wrongful act of the defendant.*"

These are sufficient citations to show that the proposition for which I contend is sound law. But in this case the damages of the plaintiff are the more clearly apparent, and real, because the defendant had notified plaintiff by telegram that they could not find the plaintiff's wheat, and that plaintiff had better come and look after it. And plaintiff, in obedience to this request, did try to find the wheat, and did incur expenses in doing so, and it is clear that the plaintiff did not and has not recovered the possession of all the wheat, or its value, to the extent of the unpaid time drafts, and is out of pocket the freight money, and the costs and expenses of the freight suits and the trover suits.

If, then, the actual possession of the wheat, or its value to the extent of the unpaid drafts would not abate or bar the action for damages occasioned by the wrongful acts or defaults of defendant and its agent, with how much more reason should the right of action remain intact, not abated or barred, when the plaintiff has neither possession of the wheat or its value to the extent of the unpaid drafts, and all these costs and charges necessarily incurred and the freight money unpaid, and with how much more reason should the mere fact that the plaintiff has or might have a clear and undisputed right of action against third parties, claiming title in good faith by purchase from A. F. Smith & Co., not operate to either abate or bar the action?

I conclude, therefore, that although the plaintiff still holds the legal title of the wheat, and could recover it or its value of third parties, that the cause of action of plaintiff against defendant for its torts and the torts of its agents, A. F. Smith & Co., is still valid, and is neither abated or barred by any act of the plaintiff, and the damages are still unmitigated to the extent of the unpaid drafts and interest, the unpaid freight money, the costs and expenses of searching after the property, and the costs and expenses of the trover suits and the suits of the vessel owners to recover the freight. These are all damages sustained by the wrongful acts and defaults of defendant and its agents.

The question in the case then is not whether A. F. Smith & Co. did, or did not obtain a valid title to the wheat, nor whether their vendees did or did not obtain a valid title to the wheat. The question in the case is whether the defendant obeyed all of the instructions of the plaintiff, or done, or omitted to do any acts proper and necessary to be done to protect the plaintiff, and if it did not obey instructions or was guilty of any act of omission or commission, whether the plaintiff has sustained any damages by reason thereof.

The plaintiff claims, not only, that its instructions were violated and utterly disregarded by defendant, and that it, in consequence thereof, has sustained great damages, but that the defendant was an active participator in the fraud of A. F. Smith & Co.

1st. The plaintiff claims that the jury might legally find from the evidence that the defendant intended and designed to place the two cargoes of wheat of the plaintiff into the control of A. F. Smith & Co., so that they could and would immediately sell and ship the same, and apply the proceeds to payments of other indebtedness than the time drafts of plaintiff, and that A. F. Smith & Co. did immediately ship the wheat and convert the proceeds to their own use.

That the defendant combined and colluded with A. F. Smith & Co. to deliver the two cargoes of wheat of the plaintiff to A. F. Smith & Co. for immediate sale and shipment before maturity of the unpaid time drafts, could and might have been "properly found by the jury," (had the question been left to them,) from the following facts, (with other facts in the record not herein specially noted,) to-wit:

1st. The cargoes, immediately on arrival, were sent directly to the warehouse of A. F. Smith & Co.

2d. No personal attention was given to the delivery of the cargoes, and no inquiry was made by the defendant as to the disposition of the cargoes after the order of delivery was endorsed on the back of the captains' bills of lading. No inquiry was made as to whether the cargoes were delivered in accordance with the terms of the order of delivery, and no receipt, writing or voucher of any kind was delivered to or received by the defendant showing that the wheat was delivered into the Corn Exchange Elevator for the account of T. L. Baker, cashier, subject to the order of defendants. No diligence whatever was used by defendants to ascertain whether its order of delivery had ever been obeyed. In fact it was not obeyed. The wheat was never stored at all in the Corn Exchange Elevator It was shipped away, as fast as it was unloaded. It was "spouted" direct from the vessels, through the Corn Exchange Elevator into canal boats, and shipped to New York and other points. And these shipments might have been seen by simply looking out of the bank window.

3d. The Corn Exchange Elevator was in plain view of the bank and the shipping of the wheat was in plain view of the defendant and was openly and publicly done.

At folio 210 the Cashier says, "there is nothing between the north window of the bank and the Corn Exchange Elevator to intercept the view of the elevator, unless it is vessels. I could see a vessel and canal boat at the Corn Exchange Elevator if there were no vessels lying outside of the elevator, and could see the elevator working taking out the cargo from the vessel, if the elevator was open so that I could see the movement. Don't think I could see the whole of the Corn Exchange Elevator without putting my head outside of the window. I could not tell whether the same grain was going into a canal boat, *but could see that the leg of the elevator was in one, and the spout of the elevator was in the other.*"

4th. The cargoes of the Atwater and D. G. Fort were mostly "spouted" directly from the vessel into the Corn Exchange Elevator and then into canal boats, and this was openly and publicly done.

5th. The cargoes were all thus shipped and disposed of *on the very day of their delivery under the orders of delivery given by the defendant.*

6th. The cargoes were entered *on the books of the elevator for the account of A. F. Smith & Co.*

7th. The very certificates of insurance delivered to Mannering by A. F. Smith & Co. described the property, "On grain *their own* or held by them on commission, or sold but not delivered." (folio 63.) They did not insure the wheat for plaintiff, or for the defendant. The wheat was insured for A. F. Smith & Co.

8th. That Bickford, of A. F. Smith & Co., on the very day of the delivery, and on the very day a deposit of $12,675 was made by A. F. Smith & Co. with defendant, applied to defendant for money to pay the freight on the two cargoes and could not get it. His request was refused.

9th. That the officers of the bank had actual knowledge as early as the afternoon of the 16th of October, that the wheat had been shipped by A. F. Smith & Co., and did not notify the plaintiff of the fact until the 19th of October, and then sent them the untruthful telegram, "*We stored the wheat for your account subject to our order, we cannot find it.*" (Folio 73.)

10th. The peculiar treatment Mr. Hayden, the agent of plaintiff, received at the hands of the officers of the bank, on his arrival at Oswego, and the untruthful statement of the President of defendant, that the wheat had been stored for the plaintiff's account. It had not been stored; his statement was false. The wheat had been shipped and was never stored.

11th. The large sum of money drawn out of defendant's bank by A. F. Smith & Co., on the 9th,—the very day of the shipment of the wheat into canal boats, being $11,500, and the freight *not paid*, and defendant refusing to let A. F. Smith & Co. have money to pay the freight.

12th. The large credit of checks on the 9th, being the sum of $12,675.00.

13th. The fact that the shipments into the canal boats were made openly; "*Any one could have seen the shipments who chose to look*," (folio 189.)

14th. The utter disregard of the letters of instruction which distinctly advised the defendant that "*A. F. Smith & Co. would pay all expenses.*"

15th. The collection of the $2,875.55 for the plaintiff on other drafts and the wrongful and persistent withholding the same until the freight money was paid.

16th. *The neglect to take warehouse receipts, or any voucher from any one, or to inquire, or to do any act to see that the wheat was actually stored in the warehouse in accordance with the terms of the order of delivery.*

17th. The utter inability of the President of the defendant, and who personally did the business, to tell the name of a single party or person upon whom the checks were drawn which were credited to A. F. Smith & Co., in the ledger account of defendant to the amount of over $20,000, within the *ten days* prior to and including the 9th day of October. It is incredible that such an officer could be so utterly ignorant of such facts.

18th. The fact that such a monstrous fraud was perpetrated by A. F. Smith & Co. and the officers of defendant having such large financial transactions and dealings with A. F. Smith & Co., and yet so utterly ignorant! It is impossible.

19th. That the draft of Smith, Wemple & Co. for $10,250 payable to the order of John Taylor & Sons which appears on the credit side of the ledger as due on October 16th, was taken at the time and in the manner as stated by the President of the defendant.

20th. The fact that on the 11th of October an acceptance of that firm of $10,173.25 was charged up by the Fourth National Bank. There is no evidence to show that it is not in fact the same draft that the defendant received. The amounts, however, appear to be different. If it is really the same draft then it is plain that the money which paid it might have been received from the cargoes of the Atwater and Fort. The drafts drawn on the 9th would certainly reach New York city in due course of mail on the 10th and would be paid by the 11th.

21st. The fact that such large sums of money were paid by A. F. Smith & Co. to both the Merchants' Bank, and the defendant at and about the time the eight cargoes of wheat arrived in Oswego, in connection with the *immediate shipment* of said cargoes before the time drafts matured.

22d. The fact that the Cashier of the defendant pretends that he did not understand the words in plaintiffs' letters of instruction, "*A. F. Smith & Co. will pay all expenses,*" to mean or include the payment by A. F. Smith & Co. of freight from Milwaukee to Oswego, and more particularly, after freight had been paid by A. F. Smith & Co. on the two shipments, one in July, 1869, and one in September, 1869, and when the precise words "*Smith & Co. will pay all expenses,*" were used in the letters of instruction accompanying these shipments, (See letters pages 57 and 58,) and that, too, when he told the captains that A. F. Smith & Co. would pay the freight, and when he knew that it was the custom in Oswego for the purchaser to pay the freight.

These, and various facts and circumstances in the record, bearing more or less on the question of fraud, were all competent evidence on the several points on which the plaintiff specifically asked to be permitted to go to the jury, and from which the jury might properly find a fraudulent intent and design on the part of defendant to place the cargoes in the possession of A. F. Smith & Co. for immediate shipment without payment of the time drafts.

Certainly this evidence strongly tends to show manifest collusion between the defendant and A. F. Smith & Co. in the delivery of the wheat, and these many and combined circumstances and facts are much stronger and more convincing evidence of the real purpose of defendant than the mere assertions or denials of the interested parties. It is said, and probably truthfully, that circumstances will not lie.

This Court, in *Castle vs. Bullard*, 23d Howard, 187, lays down, with marked and emphatic clearness, the rule which should govern the weight of circumstantial evidence. "*Circumstances altogether inconclusive, if separately considered may, by their number and joint operation, especially when corroborated by moral coincidences, be sufficient to constitute conclusive proof.*" And so I say here, that all the above various points of fact when taken in connection and together, were proper for the consideration of the jury in determining whether there was not an actual intent and design on the part of the defendant to violate the well and clearly written instructions of the plaintiff, by allowing said wheat to go into the control of A. F. Smith & Co. for immediate shipment, and to allow them to immediately ship the wheat, obtain the money thereon, and appropriate that money to the payment of indebtedness they owed the defendant, and other parties, and not to the payment of the plaintiff's drafts. The written orders uncontradicted by any other proof might be conclusive of their good faith and honest intentions. But when the written orders are shown to be only a cloak or cover, and all the facts clearly show a purpose or design at variance with the terms of the written orders, then the jury are to be the judges of the facts, and they alone are the judges. The Court cannot pass arbitrarily upon doubtful and disputed questions of fact.

In *Weide vs. Insurance Companies*, 11th Wallace, 440, the Court allowed a wide latitude of evidence to show facts upon which to raise *a fair presumption of a fact*, and it was held "*that a jury can infer the existence of a fact from another fact that is proved and most usually accompanies it.*" Now in this case, as in the Weide case, the plaintiff might not be able to contradict by direct evidence the oft-repeated assertions of the officers of defendants that they knew nothing of the fraud of A. F. Smith & Co., and that they acted in good faith, and yet it is insisted by the plaintiffs, that *such a series of facts and circumstances*, not controverted, or explained, as are shown in this record, might well and properly lead the jury to the conclusion that the officers of defendant while very particular to write out words indicating good intentions and a *bona fide* effort to obey instructions, under cloak of that apparent coloring of good faith really intended and designed to so place the wheat in possession of A. F. Smith & Co., as to successfully enable them to do with the wheat just what was done.

The cases of *Elwood vs. Telegraph Co.*, 45 N. Y., 549, *Kavanagh vs. Wilson*, 70 N. Y. 178, and *Brooklyn C. R. Co. vs. Strong*, 75 N. Y. 592, are full to the point that the jury are not bound to accept as true the direct or positive evidence of an interested witness when his positive and direct statements are contradicted or impeached by all the facts and circumstances of the case. In other words the facts and circumstances may contradict the positive evidence of the witness, and if they do the jury, and not the Court, must find the fact.

And so I repeat, that however much the officers of the defendant may testify to their good faith—their diligence—their intention to simply store the wheat for the account of the cashier of the plaintiff, subject to their order until the drafts were paid, and their pretended *innocent misapprehension* of very plain letters of instructions, yet the jury were at liberty to find from all of the testimony in the case (and should have been permitted to find) just what their real intentions and designs were as manifested by their actions and conduct. Their actions and conduct are much better evidence than their words, and where they conflict with their words the case is a proper one for the jury to find what was their real intent.

Now in this case there is evidence sufficient to warrant and justify any impartial jury in finding that all of the form of words in the writings was a mere pretext and design on the part of defendants to cover up their *real intentions* which were to so place the wheat that A. F. Smith & Co. could and would ship it and realize the money thereon, and then use the money to pay defendant and others and not pay the drafts of the plaintiff.

And is there, or can there be, any rational doubt that just what was done by A. F. Smith & Co. was just what the defendant intended and wanted A. F. Smith & Co. to do? Does anyone doubt that the officers of the defendant well knew, or at least ought to have known, just what was doing and being done by A. F. Smith & Co. with this wheat? Were they really as ignorant of the large shipments of wheat by A. F. Smith & Co., prior to October 9th and on the 9th as they claim to be? Does any sane man believe that, in a small city like Oswego, such large shipments could go on day after day without being common talk on the street, and such sharp, shrewd business men, as the officers of the defendant appear to be, not know the fact? And more particularly so when such large shipments could be plainly seen from the windows of the bank?

At least are not all these series of facts and circumstances of sufficient weight to go to a jury? *Do they conclusively establish good faith?* Are they not on the contrary evidence of bad faith? It does not seem to require any argument on the uncontradicted and undisputed facts of this case, to show that the whole proceedings of the officers of defendant was a studied, carefully prepared plan, NOT TO KNOW what might have easily been known, what the most artless, simple-minded, verdant business man, in a matter involving over $30,000 of property, would have known, to-wit: *that the cargoes of wheat as fast as received into the elevator were being shipped into canal boats.* And certainly the facts, if not evidence of fraud, collusion, and bad faith, were at least evidence of *gross neglect of duty.* Had A. F. Smith & Co. and the defendant been jointly sued for tortiously and wrongfully confederating and combining to ship this wheat and to convert the proceeds to their own use it would seem as if the series of facts and circumstances we have referred to, with others not alluded to, but in the record, would properly authorize and clearly justify a jury in finding each of them guilty.

It is certain the wheat was never stored but was immediately shipped. It is certain that the time drafts were not paid before the shipment. It is certain that the shipment was open and notorious and within plain sight of the officers of the bank. It is certain that large shipments had been going on for days prior to the 9th of October. It is certain that large checks were drawn by A. F. Smith & Co. on defendant on the very day of shipment of the wheat. It is certain that large amounts in checks were also deposited with defendant. It is certain that Bickford, of A. F. Smith & Co., applied to the defendant for money to pay the freight on the two cargoes of wheat and that his request was refused. It is certain that the defendant made no inquiry as to the wheat after it wrote the order of delivery on the captains' bills of lading, and that it knew on the afternoon of the 16th, that the wheat was or had been shipped, and did not notify plaintiff until the 19th, and it is reasonably certain that with *any inquiry* defendant could have known the fact of the shipments on the 9th. It is certain the telegram sent on the 19th of October was not truthful. It is certain that the statement of the President to Hayden, the agent of the plaintiff, that they had stored the wheat for the account of the plaintiff was false and he must have known its falsity. It is certain that the defendant collected for plaintiff $2,875.55 on other drafts in no way connected with these shipments, and withheld the same until the plaintiff paid the freight money, and the payment of which freight defendant should have made a condition of delivery of the cargo to A. F. Smith & Co. And it is certain that plaintiff by reason thereof has sustained great damage and has lost large sums of money besides being put to large and heavy bills of expense. *These are certainly undisputed facts in this record.*

I conclude, therefore, that the record shows a very plain case for a jury. The judge could not arbitrarily say, as a question of law that defendant was entirely blameless in the matter, and that plaintiff had suffered no damage. There are too many pregnant facts—facts so marked and striking in their character, and so many of them, too, *and which are uncontradicted and unexplained*, to enable the judge to say, without hesitation, or doubt, as a simple question of law, *that plaintiff had sustained no legal damage by the wrongful acts of the defendant.* It is plain that if so simple an act as taking a warehouse receipt had been done, A. F. Smith & Co. would never have dared, under the laws of New York, to sell or ship the wheat. Such a shipment, under such circumstances, would have been not only wrongful and fraudulent, but criminal. Had any officer of defendant made ANY *inquiry* during the delivery of the cargoes to ascertain whether this wheat was being delivered according to the terms of the delivery orders the sale and shipment could not have been made. Had any officer inquired into the reason of Bickford trying to raise money to pay the freight on the cargoes, they would have learned facts of great significance and importance.

It is idle to now speculate on what *might* have been. The officers of the defendant were in fault, grievous fault, in not taking the most commonplace steps to know what was being done with over $30,000 in value of property committed to their care. It is not saying too much, upon the undisputed facts of the case, to affirm that the officers of defendant *did not want to know where the wheat was, or in what condition it was.* They designedly placed the wheat so that A. F. Smith & Co. could do with it just what they did do with it. The defendant should be charged equally with A. F. Smith & Co. with the loss. It was clearly a deliberately concocted plan on the part of A. F. Smith & Co. to defraud.

And A. F. Smith & Co., if not directly invited by defendant to sell and ship the wheat, were silently and negligently permitted and allowed by defendant to do so.

2d. The officers of defendant, if not guilty of actual fraud and collusion with A. F. Smith & Co., were certainly guilty of gross carelessness and negligence in looking after and protecting over $30,000 in value of property.

If this Honorable Court should think the evidence in this record taken altogether, does not show, or tend to show, an intent and design on the part of the defendant to collude with A. F. Smith & Co., to place the wheat in their possession for *immediate shipment,* and with the design and expectation that they would immediately ship it, it cannot fail, I think, to find in the record clear evidence of *most gross carelessness and negligence on the part of the defendant.*

It is not necessary, in this action, to show a premeditated design and purpose to collude and conspire, with A. F. Smith & Co., to give them possession of the wheat for immediate shipment. It is enough to charge defendant if its officers were so *careless and negligent in the doing of the business* that A. F. Smith & Co. did sell and ship the wheat and misappropriate the proceeds. And certainly the facts of omission of duty by the defendant, if not the positive acts of defendant show an utter failure to exercise reasonable care and diligence.

III.

The defendant made A. F. Smith & Co. its agent to store the wheat until the drafts were paid and are in law responsible to plaintiff for the acts of A. F. Smith & Co.

If this point is well taken, then it is not at all a question of fraud, collusion or even negligence. The defendant is responsible for the wrongful acts of its own agent. The defendant selected A. F. Smith & Co. to *store this wheat for account of plaintiff subject to the order of the defendant.* The plaintiff had no choice in the selection of A. F. Smith & Co. The defendant is, therefore, legally liable to the plaintiff for *all acts of A. F. Smith & Co. in the discharge of that duty which tended to deprive or did deprive the plaintiff of the wheat before the drafts were paid.* Suppose that the cashier of the defendant had ordered the wheat into canal boats and obtained bills of lading from the captains, reciting that he was the shipper, and with such bills of lading had obtained money on the shipments by drawing drafts on the consignees named in the bills of lading, and then had shipped the wheat to the acceptors of the drafts, and had not applied the proceeds to the payment of the drafts, but had converted the same to his own use, is it not clear that the defendant would be liable for such acts of its cashier? Can there be any question of its liability for such acts?

And is it not equally liable when instead of its cashier being the guilty party the agent specially selected to receive and store the wheat does the act? It is, I think, too well settled law to be now questioned, that the defendant, having appointed A. F. Smith & Co. its agent to receive and store the wheat, is responsible for the *tortious and wrongful conversion of the wheat by its agent.*

For this wrongful act of the agent the plaintiff has a right of action against the defendant. The wrongful act of A. F. Smith & Co., the agent of defendant, is not, and cannot be disputed. This Court, in the Dows case, 1st Otto, on a similar state of facts, declared the shipment of the wheat by A. F. Smith & Co., to be not only *wrongful* but *fraudulent.* Now this *wrongful* and *fraudulent* act of the agent of the defendant of itself gives a right of recovery in this action. The evidence that the wheat was not stored in the elevator at all, but was immediately shipped, is in the record and undisputed. It is also undisputed that the defendant undertook, for a consideration paid, in the way of commissions and exchange, to collect the drafts, and to store the wheat for the plaintiff until the drafts were paid, and when paid to remit the amount of the drafts to the plaintiff. It is undisputed evidence that the defendant entered upon the performance of its duty by presenting the sight drafts to A. F. Smith & Co., for payment, and the time drafts for acceptance; that the defendant retained in its control the bills of lading; that the defendants elected A. F. Smith & Co. as its agents to receive and store the wheat for account of the cashier of plaintiff, subject to the order of the defendant until the drafts were paid, and that its agents A. F. Smith & Co., forthwith *and immediately, without storing the wheat at all,* sold and shipped the wheat and converted the proceeds to their own use. These are undisputed facts. These are *stipulated facts* in the record.

Now on these undisputed and stipulated facts the plaintiff insisted upon a right to recover the value of the wheat shipped to John Wilmot, at least to the extent of the unpaid time drafts, or if not all that damage at least the reasonable costs, charges and expenses which plaintiff had been put to, to obtain the said wheat or its value; and also the freight money which by the wrongful act of defendant the plaintiff had been obliged to pay, and the costs and expenses of the freight suits.

This request was denied, and not only denied, but the jury were told, that upon all of these facts *the plaintiff had no right of action.*

The law wisely and properly holds corporations to the exercise of the same degree of responsibility for the acts of its agents and officers that it imposes upon individuals. "Corporations," says Justice Swayne. in Merchants' Bank vs. State Bank, 10 Wallace, 645, "are liable for the acts of their servants while engaged in the business of their employment, in the same manner and to the same extent that individuals are liable under like circumstances."

"And it is no longer an open question in this court that corporations are liable for every wrong of which they are guilty, and in such cases the doctrine of *ultra vires* has no application." See also National Bank vs. Graham, 10th Otto, page 699.

As to the general question of the liability of a bank receiving collections, for its own neglect or failure of duty, and its liability for the acts of agents it selects, we need only cite the case of *Hoover, assignee, vs. Wise.* 1st Otto, 308 and the cases cited in the opinion.

IV.

I suppose that it is enough to secure a reversal of this case if it shall be made to appear that there was sufficient evidence to go to the jury from which the jury might properly find that the plaintiff had a legal right of action against the defendant for the wrongful acts, neglect, or default of its officers, or of its chosen agents, A. F. Smith & Co.

But as there are important questions, and fairly in the record, as to the damages plaintiff, if entitled to recover at all, should or ought to recover, and as these questions will necessarily come before the trial judge, in case a new trial is ordered, it may not be deemed impertinent to ask this Court to express its opinion on this writ of error *upon the question of the measure of damages.*

One theory of the defendants is (and was at the trial) that conceding a cause of action existed or was proven against the defendant *the damages sustained by the plaintiff were merely nominal.* This is not the view the plaintiff entertains. If there is any evidence in this record which would justify an impartial jury in finding a verdict for the plaintiff then it is clear from the record that the plaintiff has sustained real and substantial damages.

I claim that, on the assumption that the defendant has been guilty of bad faith, neglect, or omission of duty, or that it is legally liable for the acts of A. F. Smith & Co. its agent, the plaintiff is entitled to recover as *damages:*

1st. The value of the wheat wrongfully shipped by A. F. Smith & Co. to John Wilmot, at least to the extent of the unpaid time drafts.

It must be admitted that the shipment of the wheat by A. F. Smith & Co. was not only wrongful and tortious, but fraudulent.

The loss, therefore, to the plaintiff, *prima facie, is the value of the wheat at least to the extent of the unpaid time drafts, and interest from the time of the shipment.*

This was decided to be the measure of damages for the conversion of the wheat by the *innocent vendees* of A. F. Smith & Co. in the case of Dows vs. National Exchange Bank, 1st Otto, 637. It was conceded in that case that Dows & Co. were innocent purchasers, that they bought the wheat of A. F. Smith & Co. in good faith and paid a full and adequate compensation for it. And yet it was held that they acquired no title to the wheat, as against the plaintiff in the suit, and must pay the plaintiff its full value, at least to the extent of the unpaid time drafts, with interest.

In the case of the *Stearine, &c. Co. vs. Heintzman,* 112 Eng. Com. Law, page 55, the company was instructed not to let the goods go out of their possession until certain drafts were paid. The instructions were not obeyed. Suit was brought against the company, and the Court say, on page 68, "In coming to the conclusion that there was evidence on which the jury might find that the contract was made in substance as alleged, we have in effect decided that there was also evidence on which they might find that the breach was proved. It also follows, in our opinion, that the jury were right in giving *the value of the goods which were lost to the plaintiff,* and the expenses incurred by them in respect to the bill of exchange for the price, drawn according to the terms of the letter of the 19th of June."

2d. The "damages" were not diminished by reason or on account of the trover suit by plaintiff against John Wilmot, nor by reason or on account of any understanding or agreement between the plaintiff and Wilmot that trover and not replevin should be brought.

A judgment in the trover suit *without satisfaction* is no bar to an action against the defendant for its tort. The plaintiff has a right of action against *each tort feasor*, for his or its wrongful act. It can, of course, have but one satisfaction. But until it is fully satisfied a judgment against an independent tort feasor for the same tort will be no bar to an action against another tort feasor.

In *Lovejoy vs. Murray*, 3d Wallace, page 10, Justice MILLER discusses this question and on page 13, quotes from Lord Ellenborough as follows: "A judgment recovered in any form of action is still but a security for the original cause of action *until it be made productive in satisfaction to the party, and, therefore, till then it cannot operate to change any other collateral concurrent remedy which the party may have*." The learned Justice then proceeds to review the American decisions, and finally reaches the conclusion that, "in reference to the doctrine that the judgment alone vests the title of the property converted in the defendant, we have seen that it is not sustained by the weight of authorities in this country. It is equally incapable of being maintained on principle."

We cannot quote in detail the argument of the learned Justice. But on page 16, he quotes the language of Chief Justice GIBSON, as follows: "A plaintiff is not compelled to elect between actions that are consistent with each other. Separate actions against a number who are severally liable for the same thing or against the same defendant on distinct securities for the same debt or duty are concurrent remedies. Trespass is in its nature joint and several. And in separate actions against joint trespassers being consistent with each other, *nothing but satisfaction by one will discharge the rest*."

And this the plaintiff says is the law of this case. It could sue Wilmot in a separate suit in trover for the conversion of the wheat. It could also sue A. F. Smith & Co. separately in the same form of action and at the same time, and while each of these suits were pending it could sue the defendant for its wrongful acts, neglects, omissions, or for the wrongful acts of the agent it selected to take charge of this same wheat. Each suit would be independent of the other, and nothing short of a voluntary release, actual payment, or satisfaction of one suit, would abate the other.

And what is true of the bringing of the three separate suits would apply to the agreement not to bring a replevin suit. The defendant was not damnified by that agreement. Such agreement was not payment or satisfaction. The plaintiff in making that agreement had done no act to prevent the defendant from receiving the value of the wheat from its agents, A. F. Smith & Co., or the wheat from John Wilmot. The defendant was not a party to the agreement. The trover suit nor the agreement did not prevent the defendant from taking any and all steps it chose to take to obtain possession of the wheat, or to sue A. F. Smith & Co. or John Wilmot. It was as free to act *after* as it was *before* the agreement was made or the suits were brought. And as we have seen nothing but a voluntary release of its right of action by the plaintiff, or full satisfaction by some or all the other tort feasors, would or could discharge the defendant from liability.

This plaintiff, so far from doing any act, which defendant did or could rely upon, as an estoppel, gave defendant written notice of what it had done, and what it proposed to do. The defendant has, therefore, no ground upon which to predicate an estoppel. The defendant did no act, and it neglected to do no act, by reason or on account of anything done or said by the plaintiff.

It does not appear that the action of the officers of the defendant was in any respect whatsoever influenced by the agreement of plaintiff with Wilmot. In fact it was impossible that they should in any way be "influenced" by the "agreement," as they were utterly ignorant of it. Any act, therefore, which they could, might or would have done to protect the defendant was not prevented by the agreement.

It is plain, therefore, that defendant has done no act, or omitted to do any act, by reason or on account of the agreement. And certainly the officers of the defendant were in no way or manner influenced to do or to omit to do *anything to the damage* of the defendant, by reason of the agreement. The "agreement" not to bring replevin, and the actually bringing of trover instead of replevin, are, therefore, facts entirely and utterly foreign to the merits of this action. So long as the defendant was entirely ignorant of the agreement, and did not in any respect whatever, change, modify or alter its position, or its line of conduct, and was in no way injured or damnified by reason or on account of the agreement, it must be clear that the defendant has no legal right to plead the agreement either in abatement or in bar of this action, or even to allege it in mitigation of damages. And, perhaps, no better illustration could be used to show the absurdity of claiming that defendant has been or was injured by the "agreement" than considering its effect as a plea either in abatement or in bar of the action.

The defendant is sued for its independent tort. It comes into court, and by way of defense, answers that an "agreement," of which it was ignorant, had been made by the plaintiff with another and independent tort feasor, that the plaintiff would not sue that tort feasor at all, or if it did sue him it should be by an action of trover instead of replevin! The plaintiff demurs to the answer. The question then is, can one tort feasor, when sued for his independent tort, plead successfully in abatement or in bar, an agreement not to sue for the same tort another tort feasor, or to sue him only in a particular form of action. It is clear that such an "agreement" is not a "satisfaction," and it is equally clear it is not a "release" of all right of action against all of the tort feasors. Now the answer to state a legal defense must show either "satisfaction" or a "release." If the answer fails to state facts showing one or the other, either satisfaction or release, it is fatally defective as an answer. Such facts in the answer then would neither abate or bar the suit.

This then, is all there is of the so-called "agreement" with Wilmot as to the wheat, and the bringing of trover instead of replevin. The plaintiff could certainly "agree" not to sue Wilmot at all. And it could certainly "agree" with him not to bring replevin but to bring trover, without, in so doing, impairing its right of action against defendant for its tort.

And what there is of force in the argument as to the agreement not being sufficient to abate or bar the action will also apply to the argument that the agreement did not, and does *not operate to mitigate the damages.*

It must not be forgotten that long before the so-called "agreement" was made, or the trover suits brought, the right of action of the plaintiff for the neglects and defaults of the defendant and its agents *had accrued!* It was long prior to the "agreement," that the defendant had sent to the plaintiff the untruthful telegram that the wheat had been stored by defendant for the account of plaintiff subject to the order of defendant, and the false statement of the President to the same effect had been made to the agent of the plaintiff, and the wheat had already been sold and shipped by the agents selected by defendant to receive and store it. No precautions whatever had been taken or used by the defendant in looking after or caring for the property. The defendant was in default. It had utterly ignored and disregarded the familiar principle of law that *"an agent, for pay, is bound to use such means, care, skill and precaution as are adequate to the due execution of his trust. He must use the ordinary diligence of a skilful and prudent man in such affairs."* (*Allen vs Suydam*, 20 Wendell, 333). A complete and perfect cause of action, therefore, existed prior to the agreement with Wilmot, in favor of the plaintiff against the defendant, not only for its own wrongful acts and defaults, but those of A. F. Smith & Co., its agents. These wrongful acts and defaults, so damaging in their results to the plaintiff, had actually occurred, and the damages to the plaintiff, by reason thereof, had actually been sustained before the "agreement" was made, or the trover suits commenced. The wheat was actually out of the possession and control of the defendant, and A. F. Smith & Co., its selected agents to receive and store it,—and the wheat had been delivered without exacting the payment of the freight.

The plaintiff then was in this position: Its time-drafts were unpaid; the freight was unpaid; *the wheat was gone;* the plaintiff, by the false and fraudulent representations of the defendant that the wheat had been stored for its account subject to its order, had been invited to come and look after the wheat. Some of these expenses had been incurred before the whereabouts of what was supposed to be the plaintiff's wheat was ascertained. Without the aid of defendant, and at its own expense, and after some delay, the plaintiff found what it supposed and believed was its wheat in canal boats on their way to New York City. Under these circumstances, in order *to make sure of the identity of the wheat* (which it was difficult and might be impossible to identify by legal evidence) it agreed, in consideration, that the identity of the wheat should be admitted by Wilmot, it might remain in his hands without replevy, and that he should be sued therefor in trover.

Now, how was the defendant damnified or injured by this act? It had taken no steps, and did not propose to take any steps to recover the wheat. It could not be recovered by the plaintiff without giving large bonds, and bringing separate suits against each canal boat owner. The plaintiff had no legal evidence that the wheat it had discovered in these canal boats was its wheat. It could, at the best, only *guess* that it was or might be its wheat. The expenses of several replevin suits were or would be large. There was great doubt and uncertainty as to the final results of the replevin suits. There was nothing said or done by the plaintiff by which the defendant was prevented from taking any and every step and proceeding it saw fit to take to indemnify or to protect itself. It, however, never proposed to take, and it never did take any steps whatever to protect itself or the plaintiff. It offered no bonds or security for a replevin. It could, and in fact it ought to have been prompt, active and energetic to ascertain *where the wheat was, and to replevy it.* This was its plain duty. It was what the Bank did in the case of *Heiskell vs. Farmers & Merchants' Nat. Bank,* 89th, Pa. State, 156. That Bank, although it had not directed the cotton to be delivered into the hands of the acceptors of the drafts, (and which it was instructed to hold until payment of the drafts), yet, on learning that the cotton had been delivered into the hands of the acceptors *without payment of the drafts*, at once *took immediate steps to recover it, and did recover it.* It did not wait for the holders of the drafts to act. It acted promptly to save itself and its principal. But in our case, the defendant, by the neglects and defaults of its officers and agents, lost the control and possession of the wheat of the plaintiff before payment of the time-drafts, and then, with utter indifference, neglected to search after, or to find the wheat, or to regain possession or control of it. And not only that, but now claims that plaintiff shall not recover any damages against itself because, forsooth, the plaintiff did not, at once, *without legal evidence of the identity of the wheat*, institute a replevin suit against Wilmot instead of a trover suit, and made the agreement it did with Wilmot. Who can say that the plaintiff could have legally identified the wheat as its wheat, but for the agreement with Wilmot that he would admit its identity? Who can even now say that judgments would have ever been recovered, even in the trover suits, if plaintiff had been driven to *strict legal proof of identity?* It must be conceded that without the identity of the wheat being established, plaintiff had no right of action against Wilmot, either in trover or replevin.

I think this argument is conclusive on this question, and conclusively demonstrates that defendant is in no position to claim anything even in mitigation of damages because of the agreement with John Wilmot, or the bringing of trover against him instead of replevin.

It is clear, that defendant being no party to the agreement, had left to it, any and all remedies it saw fit to adopt, to save and protect itself from damages, and certainly plaintiff was not legally obliged to incur large expenses, upon doubtful and uncertain evidence of identity, to protect or indemnify defendant against liability for what must be conceded to *be a valid cause of action already accrued for the full value of all the wheat, at least to the amount of the unpaid time-drafts.*

And it may be further argued that it was the duty of the defendant, after being notified of the bringing of the trover suits, if opposed to that form of action or proceeding, to have expressed, within a reasonable time, its dissent. Certainly it should not now be permitted to say that the action of the plaintiff was in any way detrimental to its interests. It should not be allowed to remain passive after notice, until too late to change, and then to have the same benefit, as if it had promptly repudiated the act. The refusal of the defendant, after notice, to repudiate the acts of plaintiff, must undoubtedly raise a presumption that it approved of what the plaintiff was doing, as far as the notice informed it, and, in the absence of anything to rebut that presumption, the defendant must be regarded as having consented to and approved of the line of conduct adopted by plaintiff. Their silence must now be treated as a ratification and approval of the conduct of the plaintiff. (*Field vs. Farrington*, 10 Wal. 148).

It appears that, by the laws of New York, the plaintiff in order to replevy the wheat from John Wilmot would have been obliged to give bonds with resident sureties to the amount of double the value of the property. This of itself would excuse the plaintiff from bringing that form of suit.

It is certain that the plaintiff was under no legal obligation to do this in order to save harmless the defendant for its wrongful conduct or the wrongful conduct of its agents. It was in the power of the defendant, if it saw fit to do so, to incur such liability and to run such risks. It certainly can not assert that it was the bounden duty of the plaintiff to do, what the defendant, *to protect itself*, did not, and would not do. And so long, therefore, as the plaintiff has done no act and said no word to deceive or mislead the defendant, or to lead the defendant to do or omit to do any act to protect itself, the defendant, standing, as it does, under legal liability to plaintiff, not only for its own acts and defaults but those of its agents, cannot and will not be heard to say that the neglect or failure of the plaintiff to pursue one wrong-doer, or to pursue that wrong-doer in one particular form of action rather than another, has forfeited its right to substantial damages against the defendant for its own wrongful or tortious acts.

The plaintiff was certainly under no obligation to sue John Wilmot at all, in any form of action, to mitigate the damages against the defendant for its wrongful act. Much less was the plaintiff obliged to sue John Wilmot in replevin and give large bonds in a foreign jurisdiction, the liability on which depended upon unsettled and doubtful questions of law and fact. The law imposed no such duty on the plaintiff in order to protect or save harmless the defendant.

If this line of argument is sound then the measure of damages in this action is the value of the wheat which was received by John Wilmot, as well by the wrongful acts and omissions of defendant, as the wrongful acts of A. F. Smith & Co., its agents, who were selected by defendant to store the wheat for the account of the plaintiff until the drafts were paid.

2d. Not only was the plaintiff entitled to recover the value of the wheat wrongfully and fraudulently shipped by A. F. Smith & Co., the selected agents of the defendant, to take charge of and store the wheat for the account of T. L. Baker, cashier, subject to defendant's order, but also all the reasonable costs, charges and expenses of the trover suits.

In bringing the trover suits and prosecuting them to final judgment, the plaintiff was actuated by nothing but the best of motives.

It sought to recover the value of the wheat wrongfully shipped. *It duly notified the defendant of the bringing of the suits and tendered the prosecution of the suits.* The effect of this notice on the defendant is to make *the judgment conclusive evidence against the defendant of the conversion of the wheat.* The judgment certainly establishes the facts to be that Hughes, Hickox & Co., and Wilmot, although innocent purchasers of the wheat from A. F. Smith & Co., as against the plaintiff, acquired no title to the wheat by the acts of A. F. Smith & Co., and were guilty of a conversion of the wheat. *Robbins vs. Chicago*, 4th Wallace, 657.

The defendant being also liable to the plaintiff for not only the wrongful acts and omissions of itself, but also the tortious and fraudulent acts of its agents, A. F. Smith & Co., and having been duly notified of the pendency of the suits, and in no wise protesting against the bringing of said suits, but by its silence approving the acts of the plaintiff, should *now be obliged to pay all the reasonable costs and expenses of the suits.*

And more especially should this be the case if this Court should hold that the bringing of the trover suit, or the agreement not to bring a replevin suit, has in any wise changed, or altered, or mitigated the measure of damages.

In *Brown vs. Hall*, 17 Com. Bench, N. S. page 501, it was held that where a broker was sued by the vendor of goods for the failure to deliver the goods, and the broker notified his principal of the suit, and then defended it *unsuccessfully*, that he could recover as part of his damages, *the expenses of the suit.* The Court say: "The action was for unliquidated damages. If the defendant in that action had abstained from offering any defense, and had paid all that the plaintiff demanded, he could not have recovered it as against his principals, if the jury would have found that a prudent man would not have adopted that course. The defendant throughout denied their liability for the breach of contract which they themselves were instrumental in causing."

It is true this case is not quite in point, but it seems to make the question of the right to recover the costs and expenses of a suit to depend upon the good faith with which they are incurred.

In our case the defendant had virtually refused to take any important step to recover this wheat or its value. It had untruthfully asserted in its telegram to plaintiff, and by the lips of its President to Mr. Hayden, the agent of plaintiff, on his arrival at Oswego, *that it had stored the wheat* in the Corn Exchange Elevator for the account of T. L. Baker, Cashier, subject to the order of the defendant. The telegram and the statement were each false. Unless the mere giving of an order to store the wheat is exactly the same thing as its actual storage, then there was not and had never been any storage of the wheat in the Corn Exchange Elevator. The officers of the Bank had also declared that *they could not find the wheat!* Under these circumstances what would a prudent man have done? Would he not have looked after the wheat? Would he not have instituted legal proceedings? And if so are not such costs and expenses, when reasonable, proper items of damage? They would have been had the suits been unsuccessful. Are they any the less so because the suit was successful?

In *Tindall vs Bell*, 11th Meeson & Welsby, 237, it is said, "that when the mischief is done, the necessary consequences of it are what a reasonable man would do under similar circumstances when he had no other judgment but his own to resort to, *and it may be one of them that he should incur litigation."*

In *Williams vs. Burrill*, 1st. Manning, Granger & Scott, 402 (50, Eng. Com. Law) it was held that defendants were bound to pay the costs of the plaintiff in defending an action of ejectment, "because the present defendant by directing a defense, admitted there was reasonable grounds for defending, and from the statement it appears that the costs in question were necessary for such defense."

In *Blyth vs. Smith*, 44th *Eng. Com Law*, page 217, it appeared that A. was sued by B. B. immediately gave notice to C., whom he claimed was liable over to him, of the pendency of the suit, and requested him to defend it. C. refused to defend, *but did not prohibit B. from defending.* B. let the case go by default except to attend on a writ of inquiry. B. then brought suit against C., and sought to recover, with his other damages, the costs of the suit. The court by TINDAL, C. J. says: "The only question now before us is whether there was any evidence for the jury, in case this point had been made at the trial, to show that *these costs were incurred with the sanction of the defendants.* He receives notice of the action, and is invited to undertake the defense, and although he refuses to do so *he does not at all prohibit the plaintiff from defending,* Under these circumstances of the case very slight evidence would have satisfied the minds of the jury that the *defendants consented to the course adopted by the plaintiffs."*

In *Howe vs. Martin, 1st Espinasse, 162*, it was held that a party sued and who had given notice of the suit to one liable over might recover the costs of defending the suit.

It would seem from these authorities that the plaintiff, in view of all the facts disclosed in the record of this case, should have been permitted to recover all the reasonable costs and expenses of the trover suits.

3d. The plaintiff was entitled to recover all its necessary costs and expences in going from Milwaukee to Oswego to look after the wheat, and for the time and money reasonably expended in the discharge of that duty.

The defendant requested the performance of this duty. Its first telegram was: "*A. F. Smith & Co. have failed, you better come here and look after your wheat.*" (folio 160). Now these expenses, whatever they were, were certainly incurred *at the request of the defendant.*

The defendant ought not to have called on the plaintiff to perform the duty at all. It was the duty of the defendant to have taken prompt and immediate action, at its own expense, to find the whereabouts of the wheat and to have obtained it, or its value.

It would seem that this proposition is too plain for argument.

4th. The plaintiff is certainly entitled to recover as part of its damages the amount legally chargeable on the wheat for the freight from Milwaukee to Oswego.

The plaintiff expressly advised the defendant by its letters of instruction *that A. F. Smith & Co. would pay all expenses.* The cashier well understood what these "expenses" were. He told the captains that A. F. Smith & Co. would pay the freight. The very usage at the port of Oswego was that A. F. Smith Co., under the circumstances, were to pay the freight. And yet the defendant *made it no condition of delivery of the wheat that the freight should be paid.* Nay more, the defendant, when requested by Bickford to let A. F. Smith & Co have money, with which to pay the freight, refused to do so. They then knew that the wheat was delivered or being delivered without the payment of the freight.

The plaintiff did not lose any of its rights by taking upon itself, at the request of defendant, the defense of the freight suits. It expressly notified the defendant *of the precise terms and conditions on which it would defend, and the defense it would interpose.* The defendant could not accept so much and such parts of these terms as it pleased *and reject the balance.* It could not say that as to so much of the acceptance as was in its favor, it would accept the offer of the plaintiff to defend and reject so much of it as was against itself.

The terms of the acceptance must be construed and interpreted together and in its entire scope and meaning. A single paragraph can not be selected out of it, and the balance rejected.

The following cases illustrate this rule of interpretation:

Bailey vs. Berry, et als. 8 Am. Law Reg. N. S., page 270.

Sally vs. Forbes, 6th Eng. Com. Law, 11.

Rich vs. Lord, 18 Pick, 324.

Matthers vs. Chicopee M. Co., 3 Robt. (N. Y.) 713.

Insurance Co. vs. Newton, 22d Wal. 32.

The plaintiff is not estopped by anything by it said or done in and about or connected with the freight-suits from claiming its full damages from the defendant for the non-observance of its letters of instruction in this regard. The plaintiff, as well as the defendant, was liable to the vessel owner for the freight. Had the plaintiff been sued by the vessel owners it could rightfully and properly have tendered the defense of the suit to the defendant. It had a legal right to have decided the question whether the freight had or had not been paid. · It could have paid the freight without suit, and still have held the defendant for the damages it had sustained by the wrongful act or default of the defendants or its agents.

The only effect of the judgments in the freight cases was to conclusively decide that *the freight had not been paid by A. F. Smith & Co.* That judgment concluded the defendant on that point. The defendant, after those judgments, could not in any suit, where that question could or might arise, *dispute that fact.* The judgments, as against the defendant, were *res adjudicata* on that question.

The plaintiff was obliged, by the action of the defendant, to litigate that question. It did litigate it, and the New York Commission of Appeals decided that *A. F. Smith & Co. had not paid the freight.*

Now, what did the plaintiff do? Under the notice served upon it, it undertook, in good faith, to establish that the freight was paid by A. F. Smith & Co. It procured sureties to go on bonds conditioned, that if the court should adjudge that the freight was not paid, the judgment should be paid.

In this effort it was defeated, and to relieve the sureties, as well as to obtain money wrongfully withheld by defendant, it paid the judgment! Did the payment release the defendant from its obligation to the plaintiff? Was the defendant released from its obligation to respond to plaintiff, for its wrongful act, by this payment under these circumstances?

I say not, and for this reason, that the freight cases were instituted by the owners of the vessels against the defendant, and the issue and the only issue in that case was, did the defendant owe the vessel owners the freight? It could not be litigated in that case and it was not litigated in that case, whether the plaintiff had a legal cause of action against defendant for *neglect of duty.*

That issue was not and could not be tried in that suit. The effect of this payment was no other or different to my apprehension than if the plaintiff had came forward to the vessel owners and said "I am liable to you for the payment of this freight and I will pay it without suit."

Is it not clear that plaintiff, by such payment, would not be estopped from asserting its right against defendant to recover damages sustained by defendant's neglect to do its duty? How have the defendants been damnified by the act of payment in the one case and not the other? What right or rights has it lost? None whatever. The only difference, as seems to me, is, that in the one case, that of paying without suit, the plaintiff would have to establish the fact by evidence that A. F. Smith & Co. had not paid the freight. In the other case, payment after judgment, *the judgment would be conclusive of the fact that A. F. Smith & Co. had not paid the freight.*

5th. The costs and expenses of defending the freight cases are also a proper item of damages.

All of the cases above cited as to a defendant being charged with costs and expenses are here directly in point and seem conclusive on this question. These expenses were incurred at the request of defendant, and on the tender by defendant of the defense of the suit, *and the defense was not successful.* This was the precise state of facts which existed in the English cases.

In *Whiting vs. The National Bank of Potsdam*, 45th N. Y., 305, the holder of a promissory note brought suit against the maker. The maker plead as a defense that the note was a forgery. The holder gave notice to his transferor of the suit, and tendered to him the defense. The defense was sustained. The holder then brought suit against his transferor on an implied warranty of title, and claimed as part of his damages the costs and expenses of his suit against the maker. It was held he could recover them. The Court say: "Whether the transferee of a note is bound to bring on action, and have an adjudication as to its validity, before he can recover of the transferor upon the implied warranty of its validity, may be doubtful, but that he is at liberty to do so, *and if defeated, may recover the costs incurred by him from his assignor is well settled.* The plaintiff is entitled to the benefit of this rule."

The following cases clearly establish the rule that where there is a legal liability over, and the party thus liable is seasonably notified of legal proceedings, and the defense or prosecution is properly tendered, the injured party may recover, as part of his damages, all the legal costs and expenses of such suit.

> *Kip vs. Brigham*, 7th Johns, 168.
> *Bennett vs. Jenkins*, 13th Johns, 50.
> *Pitcher vs. Livingston*, 4th Johns, 5.
> *Sweet vs. Patrick*, 12th Maine, 10.
> *Morlett vs. Clary*, 20th Arkansas, 263.
> *Linus vs. Peake*, 7th Taunton, 153.
> *Mons Le Blanch vs. Wilson*, 8th Com. Pleas Law Rep., 227.
> *Collen vs. Wright*, 7th E. & B., 301.
> And affirmed in 8th E. & B., 647.

The only question, then, is whether a reasonable, prudent, cautious man would, under the circumstances, have made the defense and incurred the expense.

The good faith of the plaintiff in making the defense is not and can not be questioned.

Now, each and all of these items of damage and expenses were incurred and sustained solely by and in consequence of the neglect of the defendant to obey the instructions of the plaintiff.

If these points or any of them are well taken, it follows that the plaintiff has sustained not only substantial damage, but large and heavy damages by the wrongful acts and neglect of the defendant and its selected agents, A. F. Smith & Co. And if such damages were sustained, then the direction of the learned Judge to the jury to return a verdict for the defendant is erroneous, and the judgment entered in favor of the defendant and against the plaintiff should be reversed.

H. M. FINCH,
Of Counsel for Plaintiff in Error.

Supreme Court of the United States.

THE MILWAUKEE NATIONAL BANK, OF WISCONSIN,

Plaintiff in Error,

vs.

THE CITY BANK,

Defendant in Error.

BRIEF AND POINTS

of Defendant in Error.

ALBERTUS PERRY,

Att'y and Counsel for Def't in Error.

SUPREME COURT OF THE UNITED STATES.

THE MILWAUKEE NATIONAL
BANK, of Wisconsin,
Plaintiff in Error,
versus
THE CITY BANK,
Defendant in Error.

This case is brought before this Court by writ of error to the Circuit Court of the United States, for the Northern District of New York.   Page 76.

The action was brought to recover damages, alleged to have been sustained by the plaintiff from the neglect or misconduct of the defendant, in relation to two cargoes of wheat consigned to it.   Pages 1 to 6.

Upon the trial the court ordered a verdict for the defendant, and upon that verdict judgment was entered in favor of the defendant for costs, on the 2d day of January, 1878. Pages 9, 10 and 74

The facts established upon the trial are substantially as follows :

The plaintiff was a banking corporation organized under the laws of the United States, located and doing business at Milwaukee, in the State of Wisconsin, and the defendant was a banking corporation, organized under the laws of the State of New York, and located and doing business in the city of Oswego, in that State.   Pages 2, 6, 10, 33, 53.

In the month of September, 1869, the firm of Mower, Church & Bell, commission merchants, of Milwaukee, Wisconsin, purchased at that place two cargoes of wheat for, and at the request of A. F. Smith & Co., one of which, consisting of 17,000 bushels, was shipped upon the schooner "Atwater," and the other, consisting of 17,550 bushels, was shipped on the schooner "D. G. Fort." Duplicate bills of lading of the respective cargoes were executed, one of which was signed by the master of the vessel and delivered to Mower, Church & Bell, and the other was signed by Mower, Church & Bell, and delivered to the master. The bills of lading described Mower, Church & Bell, as the shippers, and provided that the wheat should be delivered "*as addressed in the margin, or to his or their assigns or consignees, upon paying the freight or charges.*" In the margin of the bills was written: "*Account T. L. Baker to City Bank, Oswego, N. Y.*" T. L. Baker was the cashier of the plaintiff bank. Page 10, folio 38, pages 16, 17, 18, 44, 59, 49.

Mower, Church & Bell, paid for the wheat with their own funds, and on receiving the bill of lading of the "Atwater," they drew two drafts on A. F. Smith & Co., dated September 27th, 1869, one at 30 days, for $15,000, and the other at sight for $5,085.43. On receipt of the bill of lading of the "D. G. Fort," they drew on A. F. Smith & Co., two other drafts, dated September 29th, 1869, one at 30 days, for $17,000, and one at sight for $4,052.62. They presented the drafts, with the respective bills of lading attached, to the plaintiff for discount, and the plaintiff discounted them in the usual course of business upon the faith and credit of the bills of lading. At the same time they delivered to the plaintiff certificates of the insurance of the wheat for the voyage, which had been procured and paid for by them. Pages 16 and 17.

Invoices of the purchase of the wheat were sent by them to A. F. Smith & Co., but no bill of lading was sent to the latter by any one. Pages 15, 16, 19, 28, (Folios 60 and 83.)

The plaintiff, after discounting the drafts, endorsed them as follows: "Pay D. Mannering, cash, or order, for collection on account, Milwaukee National Bank of Wisconsin, T. L. Baker, cashier," and enclosed them with the bills of lading and certificates of insurance, in letters to the defendant, as follows :

Milwaukee, September 29th, 1869.

D. MANNERING, ESQ., CASHIER,

DEAR SIR:

I inclose for collection and remittance to National Park Bank, N. Y., bills as stated below.

A. L. Smith & Co., sight $5,085.43,

A. F. Smith & Co., 30th October, $15,000,

B. F. Schooner "Atwater" 17,000 bushels wheat in Ætna Insurance Company, 11,250 ; Home Ins. Co., 10,000. Cer. weight and inspection. Please hold above certificates insurance for arrival of vessel, and on the wheat going into store, please have it insured for enough to cover drafts. On payment of the drafts you will please deliver the cargo to order of Messrs. Smith & Co. If not paid please hold and advise me by telegraph. Messrs. Smith & Co., will pay all expenees. Truly Yours,

T. L. BAKER,

Cashier.

On the next day, September 30th, Baker wrote Mannering inclosing bill of lading of the Schooner "D. G. Fort," certificate of insurance, etc., saying: "The instructions given you yesterday, and on all the cargoes shipped to you for Messrs. A. F. Smith & Co., you will please apply to this."

These letters with enclosures, were duly received by the defendant, and thereupon, Mr. Mannering, the defendant's cashier, presented the drafts to Smith & Co , the sight drafts for payment, and the time drafts for acceptance. Smith & Co. paid the sight drafts, and accepted the time drafts. The defendant retained in its possession the bills of lading. Pages 17, 19, 23, 70.

The vessels, with their cargoes, arrived at Oswego, on the evening of the 8th day of October, and on the morning of the 9th, the masters reported to the defendant, and thereupon Mr. Mannering, the defendant's cashier, endorsed upon the bills of lading an order, in these words: "Deliver to the Corn Exchange Elevator, for the account of T. L. Baker, cashier, Milwaukee, subject to the order of the City Bank, Oct. 9th, 1869, D. Mannering, Cashier. Pages 19, 20, 44, 61.

The master of each vessel delivered his cargo under such order and took a receipt therefor on the back of the bill of lading, on which the order was written. Pages 20, 45, 61.

A. F. Smith & Co., were the sole lessees of the Corn Exchange Elevator. That elevator was fitted with bins and was used as a warehouse for the storage of grain; and also for the transhipment of grain from lake vessels into canal boats. It was situated on the East bank of the Oswego river, and had capacity for the storage of 250,000 bushels. There were six or seven other elevators in Oswego, three or four of which were used as flouring mills. Pages 20, 25, 52, 53.

(For a more particular description of the elevator, see Pages 56 and 58.) Upon the delivering of the wheat to the elevator, Mr. Mannering applied to Smith & Co., for additional insurance thereon, and received from them a certificate in the following form :

"A. F. Smith & Co., .:......................................$5,000.

"On grain, their own, or held by them on commission or sold, but not delivered, contained in the Corn Exchange Elevator, situated on block number 63, Second Ward, Oswego, N. Y., loss, if any, payable to the City Bank of Oswego, N. Y.

National Ins. Co., Boston Mass.,.............. ....$2,500.

Putnam Ins. Co., Hartford, Conn.,.....................$2,500.
                                                            ─────────
                                                            $5,000

For fifteen days from date,
          Oswego, Oct. 4th, 1869,
                    For above Ins. Co.,
                              W. Newkirk, Ag't."

The defendant held other insurance upon grain in the elevator, sufficient in amount with the above certificate to cover the drafts and acceptances of Smith & Co., held by the defendant, and in the policies thereof on the property was described substantially as in the above certificate. The premiums for such insurance were paid by Smith & Co. Pages 20, 26, 31, 32, 73.

On the same day on which the wheat was delivered to the Corn Exchange Elevator, (October 9, 1869), Smith & Co. sold 14,800 bushels thereof to Randall & Kenyon, and, by their direction, shipped the same upon canal boats consigned to Hughes, Hickcox & Co., at the city of New York, 7,700 bushels, on the canal boat "A. Post," and 7,400 bushels on the canal coat "P. B. Davis." Bills of lading were executed by the masters of said canal boats, and Randall & Kenyon drew their drafts upon Hughes, Hickcox & Co., against said shipments, one for $8,085.00, and one for $8,140.00, which, upon the faith and credit of the bills of lading attached thereto, were accepted and paid by Hughes, Hickcox & Co., in the usual course of business.

The purchase by Randall & Kenyon was made in good faith, as was also the acceptance and payment of the drafts by Hughes, Hickcox & Co. The payment of the drafts by Hughes, Hickcox & Co., was made twenty-six days before the arrival of the wheat, in the city of New York, and fourteen days before they had notice of the plaintiff's claim to the wheat.

The canal boats arrived in New York November 5th, 1869, and the wheat was delivered to Hughes, Hickcox & Co.. Pages 20, 21, 64.

On the 9th October, 1869, Smith & Co. shipped from the elevator of the cargo of the schooner "Atwater" 7,641 and 26-60 bushels of wheat, by the canal boat "E. N. Shepard," and consigned the same to John Wilmot, at the city of New York, and on the same day, they shipped of the cargo, of the "D. G. Fort," 7,650 bushels of wheat by the canal boat "Moses Melvin," and consigned the same to John Wilmot.

Against these shipments Smith & Co. drew their drafts upon Wilmot; one for $8,415.10, and one for $8,415.00, which drafts, upon the faith and credit of the bills of lading attached, were accepted and paid by Wilmot before the arrival of the boats or the receipt of the wheat by him. Pages 33, 64.

Smith & Co. sold and delivered to one G. Woolworth of Watertown, N. Y., of the cargo of the schooner "D. G. Fort" 2,005 bushels, and the remainder of the cargoes of the "Atwater" and "D. G. Fort" they sold and delivered to Randall & Kenyon. Page 42.

These shipments and sales by A. F. Smith & Co., had all been made prior to the 16th day of October, 1869, and on that day, which was Saturday, they suspended payment and on the same day, late in the afternoon, the defendant first learned that the wheat had been removed from the elevator. Pages 52, (fol. 149,) 55, (fol. 160,) 62, (fol. 182,) Pages 50, (fol. 145,) 72, fol. 211.)

On the 18th day of October, 1869, the defendant telegraphed to the plaintiff as follows: "A. F. Smith & Co., have failed, you better come here and look after your wheat." Page 24.

Thereupon the plaintiff sent an agent, (T. S. Hayden) to Oswego, to look after the wheat.

Hayden found the wheat, and on the 22d of October, telegraphed from Oswego to Hughes, Hickox & Co., as follows: "Seventy-seven hundred bushels of wheat shipped to you from Oswego, Oct. 10th, 1869, on canal boat 'Alanson Post,' and seventy-four hundred bushels shipped to you on the same day from Oswego, on canal boat 'P. B. Davis,' is the property of the Milwaukee National Bank, of Wisconsin, which will hold you responsible for the same." This telegram was received by Hughes, Hickcox & Co., on the same day. Pages 24, 25, 55, 56, especially page 43, (Fol. 126.)

In the fall of 1869, and before any suit was commenced by the plaintiff against either John Wilmot or Hughes, Hick cox & Co., and before the actual receipt by Hughes, Hickcox & Co., of the wheat shipped to them on the canal boats "A. Post" and "P. B. Davis," and before the actual receipt by John Wilmot of the wheat shipped to him on the boats "E. H. Shepard" and Moses Melvin," it was agreed by, and between the plaintiff, and Hughes, Hickcox & Co., and John

Wilmot, that the plaintiffs would not replevy said wheat, but would sue in trover for the value thereof, and in consideration thereof, that they, Hughes, Hickcox & Co., and John Wilmot would respectively on the trial of such actions, admit the receipt by them respectively of such wheat. Page 43.

Accordingly the plaintiff, in the fall of 1869, commenced actions of trover in the Circuit Court of the United States, for the Northern District of New York, against Hughes, Hickcox & Co., and John Wilmot to recover the value of the wheat received by them respectively. On the 28th of July, 1873, the plaintiff recovered judgment in such actions against the defendants therein; against Hughes Hickcox & Co., for $24,865 damages, and $792.04 costs, against John Wilmot, for $24,658.69 damages, and $821.40 costs. Page 42,

Hughes, Hickcox & Co., (appealed?) from the judgment against them to this Court, and pending such appeal to wit, on the 8th of March, 1876, they paid to the plaintiff, and the plaintiff accepted and received $25,000 in full satisfaction of its judgment, and discharged the same of record.

On the 28th February, 1873, G. Woolworth paid to the plaintiff and the plaintiff accepted $300, in settlement of its claim against him for the wheat received by him.

And on the 29th April, 1876, Randall & Kenyon paid to the plaintiff, and the plaintiff accepted $2,473.73, in settlement of the plaintiff's claim against them, for the wheat received by them, other than that shipped to Hughes, Hickcox & Co. Page 42.

The time drafts drawn by Mower, Church & Bell on A. F. Smith & Co., were not paid, and with the bills of lading of the cargoes of the "Atwater" and "D. G. Fort" were returned to the plaintiff. Page 24.

On the delivery of the cargoes of the "Atwater" and "D. G. Fort" at Oswego, Smith & Co. paid to the masters a portion of the freight, in currency, and gave their checks on the Fourth National Bank of New York for the remainder. Those checks were not paid, and John T. Davison and others, owners of the "Atwater," and Samuel V. Parsons and another, owners of the "D. G. Fort," brought actions in the Supreme Court of the State of New York, against the defendant, the City Bank, to collect the freight represented by the checks and recovered judgments therein.

From those judgments appeals were taken to the Court of Appeals, and the judgments were affirmed by that Court.

The plaintiff herein by its attorney, George G. French, Esq., took charge of the defence of those actions, and prosecuted the appeals, and finally paid the judgments therein, amounting in the case of Davison and others to the sum of $2,440.09, and in the case of Parsons and another to the sum of $2,040.93. Pages 43, 52, 59, 61, 35.

The value of the wheat at Oswego on the 9th October, 1869, was from $1.17 to $1.30 per bushel. Page 33.

During the year 1868, and the year 1869, up to the 16th day of October, A. F. Smith & Co. were engaged in business as grain merchants and warehousemen at the city of Oswego.

During that time their reputation for pecuniary responsibility and commercial integrity was good. Page 23, (fol. 71,) 53, (fol. 154,) 54, (fols. 157, 158,) 55, (fol. 160,) 56, (fol. 164,) 72, (fols. 210, 211.)

The wheat in question was removed from the Corn Exchange Elevator, and disposed of by A. F. Smith & Co. without the knowledge, order or permission of the defendant or any of its officers. Pages 31, (fol. 94,) 82, (fol. 95,) 57, (fols. 166, 167,) 72, (fols. 211, 212,) 73, (fol. 213.)

It was the usual course of business at the city of Oswego, in 1869, and for twenty years or more prior thereto, when grain was consigned to a bank in that city, and time drafts drawn against the grain, were sent to the bank for collection, with instructions to hold the grain until payment of the drafts, for the bank to order the grain into the warehouse of the party drawn upon, for account of the consignor and subject to the order of the bank, if such party had a warehouse. Pages 56, (fol. 165,) 58, (fol. 170,) 71.

Neither the defendant nor other of the Oswego Banks, had at any time an elevator, warehouse or place for the storage of grain.   Page 56, (fol. 164.)

No portion of the proceeds of the sales of the cargoes of the "Atwater," and "D. G. Fort," was received by the defendant.

See statement of account of Smith & Co., with defendant, from August 1st, 1869, to May 30th, 1870.   Pages 39, 40.   Also pages 42, (fol. 125,) 59, (fol. 172,) 49, (fol. 142,) 50, (fol. 144,) 65, 66, (fols. 193, 194.)

I.

The defendant, as consignee of the cargoes of wheat, shipped on the schooners "Atwater," and "D. G. Fort" was guilty of no misconduct or neglect of duty.

First—The defendant complied strictly with the instructions of the plaintiff except, perhaps, in not procuring the specific wheat to be insured.

> The exception, if any, is wholly unimportant, as no injury resulted therefrom.

The defendant did procure insurance upon grain in the Corn Exchange Elevator, payable to it, in case of loss, sufficient in amount to cover the unpaid drafts against the wheat.   (Pages 20, 26, 31, 32, 73.)

The defendant collected the sight drafts and remitted the proceeds.

It procured acceptance of the time drafts and *held* the wheat for their payment.   (Pages 18, 20.)

The defendant directed the wheat to be delivered to the Corn Exchange Elevator, *subject to its own order, and for account of the plaintiff.*

> The expression "for account of" imported that the ownership of the wheat was in the plaintiff.

Dows vs. Perrin, 16 N. Y., 325.
Dows vs. Greene, 24 Do., 638, 640.
First National Bank of Toledo vs. Shaw,
61 Do., 283, 292.
Davison vs. City Bank, 57 N. Y., 81, 86.

This was an action to recover freight on the cargo of the "Atwater." Earl Com. says : "It (this defendant) accepted the wheat by directing it to be delivered to the Elevator, subject to its order. The wheat, after such delivery, *remained under its control and it had all the possession it could take or be expected to have.*

Dows vs. National Exchange Bank, 1
Otto, 618, 633.

This case grew out of the same transactions as the case at bar, and the language of Mr. Justice Strong is directly applicable here.

He says : "The Merchants Bank (substitute City Bank) having been only special agents of the owners, had no power to make such a delivery as would divest the ownership of their principals. And they *made no attempt to divest that ownership.* They *guardedly retained the jus disponendi.*

Concurrently with their direction that the wheat should be delivered to the Elevator, in the very order for the delivery they stated that the cargoes were for the account of W. G. Fitch, cashier, (T. L. Baker, cashier), and were to be held subject to their order.

* * * They (A. F. Smith & Co.,) were informed that the holders of the drafts and bills of lading had no intention to let go their ownership so long as the drafts remained unpaid. The possession they had, therefore, was not their possession. It belonged to their bailors ; and they were mere warehousemen and not vendees."

And it was held that a subsequent sale by Smith & Co. conferred no title on the purchaser.

Farm. & Mech. Nat. Bank vs. Logan, 74
N. Y., 568.
Same Plaintiff vs. Atkinson, 74 N. Y., 587.
Same Plaintiff vs. Hazeltine, 78 N. Y., 104.

Second—The instructions of the plaintiff contemplated that the defendant was to employ a warehouseman to store the wheat.

The plaintiff, in its letter, says : "*On the wheat going into store*, please have it insured," &c., not "on receipt of the wheat," nor "On the wheat going into your warehouse." Page 18, (Fol. 56, 57.)

The defendant had no warehouse for the storage of grain. None of the Oswego banks had.

The statute of New York, under which the defendant was organized, prohibited it from holding, by purchase or lease, a warehouse for such purpose.

Laws of N. Y. 1838, chap. 260 §24, 4th Gen. Stat. of N. Y. pp 132, 133.

The 24th Section of that act provides that, "It shall be lawful for such association to purchase, hold and convey real estate for the following purposes :

1st. Such as shall be necessary for its immediate accommodation in the convenient transaction of its business, or

2d. Such as shall be mortgaged to it in good faith by way of security for loans made by, or moneys due to such association, or

3d. Such as shall be conveyed to it in satisfaction of debts previously contracted in the course of its dealings, or

4th. Such as it shall purchase at sales under judgment decrees, or mortgages held by such association.

The said association shall not purchase, hold or convey real estate in any other case or for any other purpose."

The powers of the defendant are prescribed by the eighteenth section of the act, as follows :

"Such association shall have power to carry on the business of banking, by discounting bills, notes and other evidences of debt ; by receiving deposits, by buying and selling gold and silver bullion, foreign coins and bills of exchange, in the manner specified in their articles of association, for the purposes authorized by this act ; by loaning money on real and personal security, and by exercising such incidental powers as shall be necessary to carry on such business."

The business of receiving, storing and taking care of wheat is the business of a warehouse man and in no way incidental to the business of banking.

Talmage vs. Pell, 7 N. Y., 328.

Bank Commissioners, vs. St. Lawrence Bank; 7 N. Y. 513.

Rev. Stat. of U. S., Sec. 5136, sub. 7.

Wiley vs. First Nat. Bank of Brattleboro, 47, Vt. Rep. 546.

S. C., 19 American Rep. 122.

First Nat. Bank of Lyons, vs. the Ocean Nat. Bank, 60 N. Y., 278.

The powers of the defendant being limited by a public statute, the plaintiff was chargeable, with knowledge of the limitation.

Story on Agency, §86, Owings vs. Hull, 9, Peters 607, 626.

Third—The defendant was guilty of no fault in storing the wheat with A. F. Smith & Co.

By accepting the consignment under the instructions given, the defendant became bound to place the wheat in store, with a warehouseman in good credit, and in accordance with the usual course of business at Oswego.

This obligation was fully discharged.

a. The standing of Smith & Co., as merchants and warehousemen was good—as good as that of any one in the city. Page 23, (Fol. 70) 56, (Fol. 164).

b. It was in accordance with usage which had long prevailed at Oswego, that the defendant should order the wheat into the warehouse of Smith & Co. Pages 56, (Fol. 165), 58, (Fol. 170.)

c. This usage violated no rule of law. It was reasonable and not inconsistent with the instructions of the plaintiff.

Both economy and convenience would suggest that grain, consigned as in this case, should be stored in the warehouse of the party for whom it was purchased, and ultimately intended, and who had paid part of the price, rather than in the warehouse of a stranger.

There was less antecedent probability that this wheat would be stolen if placed in the warehouse of Smith & Co. than if it had been placed in any other warehouse in Oswego.

They already had a large interest in the wheat. They had paid over $9,000 on account of the purchase price. The plaintiff's letter stated that they would pay all expenses, and on payment of the time drafts, the wheat was to be delivered to their order. (Page 18).

Under such circumstances it was highly reasonable and proper that they should be permitted to have the wheat stored in their own warehouse, rather than be compelled to pay for its storage in another.

As has been said, the plaintiff in effect, directed the defendant to procure the wheat to be stored with some warehouseman. It was left to the defendant to select the depositary according to its discretion and the usual course of business at Oswego.

d. The plaintiff must be presumed to have known of the usage and it was bound by it.

The plaintiff sent the drafts and bills of lading to the defendant in another state, and it had previously had similar transactions with Oswego banks. (Pages 27, 71.)

"Whenever the authority given to an agent is to transact business for the principal in a foreign country, or in another State, it must, in the absence of all counter-proofs, be presumed to include the authority to transact it in the forms and by the instruments and according to the laws of the place where it is to be done. And each party under such circumstances is bound to know what such forms and instruments are, and what acts are required by those laws."

Story on Agency, §86.

"Not only are the means necessary and proper for the accomplishment of the end, included in the authority, (given to the agent) but also all the various means which are *justified or allowed by the usages of trade.*"

Story on Agency, §§60, 73.

" The usages of a particular trade or business, or of a particular class of agents, are properly admissable, not indeed for the purpose of enlarging the powers of the agents employed therein, but for the purpose of interpreting those powers which are actually given; for the means ordinarily used to execute the authority are included in the power and may be resorted to by all agents, and *especially by commercial agents.*"

Story on Agency, sections 77, 96, 180.

Lloyd's Paley on Agency, (3d Ed.), 198 note.

Mollett vs. Robinson, L. R. 5, C. P. 646.

L. R. 7, C. P. 84.

In this case in 5th Law Rep. Wills J. says: "The agent may perform the business he is engaged for according to the usages of the market, in matters of detail, although the principal be unaware of such usage; became every authority to do a thing not specifying the way *implies authority to do it in a reasonable way, which the usual way prima facie is.*

1 Am. Lead Cas. (H. & W.) 683.

Owings vs. Hull, 9, Peters 607.

McKinstry vs. Pearsall, 3, Johns. 319.

Van Alen vs. Vanderpool, 6, Johns. 69.

Goodenow vs. Tyler, 7, Mass. 36.

Homer vs. Dorr, 10, Mass. 26.

Clark vs. Van Northwick, 1, Pick, 343.

Wallis vs. Bailey, 49 N. Y. 464.

1 Smiths Lead, Cas. (H. & W. notes,) 905, *et seq.*

Fourth. Had the defendant ordered the wheat into a warehouse, other than that of Smith & Co., and had it been stolen from there, it might with greater reason have been claimed that the defendant was in fault.

Not only is the agent, in the absence of instructions, authorized to act according to the customary mode of business, but it is his duty to do so, and he departs from it at his peril.

Says Story, "It may be laid down on a general rule, in the absence of his instructions, that if there be a known usage of trade, or a mode of transacting business, applicable to the particular agency or analogous to it, in such a case it. will be the duty of the agent to conform to it: and any departure from it not required by necessity, will be at the peril, of the agent, and involve him in full responsibility for any loss occasioned thereby."

Story on Agency, § 60, §§ 199, 200.
Evans vs. Potter, 2 Gall, 13.
Upton vs. Suffolk Co. Mills, 11 Cush, 586.

Metcalf J. "It is an elementary principle, that an agent employed generally to do any act, is authorized to do it *only* in the usual way of business. * * * A general agent is not, by virtue of his commission, permitted to depart from the usual manner of effecting what he is employed to effect."

Fifth—The defendant was not required to take from Smith & Co., formal warehouse receipts for the wheat.

It was not usual to exact such receipts. (Pages 28, 29, 57, 58, 62.

No complaint of the failure to do so is made in the declaration. (Pages 1, 6.

The orders of the defendant and the receipts of Smith & Co. were in substance and legal effect warehouse receipts. (Pages 20, 44, 45, 60.)

Smith & Co. thereby acknowledged the receipt of the wheat in their warehouse, as the property of the plaintiff, subject to the order of the defendant.

See First Sub. of Point I.

II.

The defendant is not responsible for the fraudulent conduct of A. F. Smith & Co., in converting the wheat to their own use.

First. The plaintiff did not contemplate that the defendant would by its own immediate officers and servants store and take care of the wheat, but, on the contrary expected that it would employ some suitable warehouseman to do so.

This is apparent from the plaintiff's letter of instructions, and from the usage of trade at Oswego.

The defendant did not contract or undertake to assume the duties and responsibilities of a warehouseman, and as such to store and care for the wheat.

So far as the physical control of the wheat was concerned, the defendant was the Attorney or personal representative of the plaintiff, to select a suitable depositary and nothing more.

When the plaintiff in its letter said "if not paid, *please hold*," and "on payment of the drafts *you will please deliver*" it, of course did not mean a physical holding and delivery, but a holding and a delivery of the legal title. It has been shown that that was done.

The defendant therefore was bound only to the exercise of good faith and ordinary diligence in the selection of a warehouseman and having discharged that duty, Smith & Co., and not the defendant are answerable to the plaintiff for the conversion of wheat.

"In many cases (says Story) a similar authority (*ie* to employ a sub-agent) arises by implication, from the conduct of the parties or from the usage of trade. * * * In all cases of this sort, the agent will not ordinarily be responsible for the negligence or misconduct of the sub-agent, if the employment of the sub-agent is authorized by the principal either expressly, or impliedly by the usage of trade on the usual dealings between himself and his principal, and he has used reasonable diligence in his choice as to the skill and ability of the sub-agent. * * * But the sub-agent will under such circumstances be himself directly responsible to the principal for his own negligence or misconduct." Story on Agency, § § 201, 217, *a.*

Lloyd's Paley on Agency, 17, 20.
Commercial Bank of New Orleans vs. Martin,
1 La. Ann., 344.

Slidell J., says: "The law is well settled that when in the course and from the nature of the business it becomes *necessary to employ sub-agents*, by reason of their particular profession or skill, the agent will not in such cases be responsible for the negligence or misconduct of the sub-agent, if he has used reasonable diligence in his choice as to skill and ability of the sub-agent."

In that case the bank had selected an attorney in Alabama to collect a note at the request of the payee.

In the case at bar, it was absolutely necessary that the defendant should select a warehouseman to take charge of the wheat.

Baldwin vs. Bank of Louisiana, 1 La. Ann, 344.
Goswell vs. Dunkley, 1 Strange 680.
The defendant received a watch and sword to sell.

He pleaded that he carried them to Porto Bello and to keep them safe put them in a warehouse of the South Sea Company, and that the warehouse was broken open and the articles taken.

On demurrer to the plea, the Court held it good, saying that if the warehouse was not a place of safe custody, that should have been replied. A robbery there was the same as from the defendant's own person, and that a bailiff for the sale of merchandise is not obliged to keep the goods always about him.

Van Wart vs. Wooley, 3 Barn & Cress. 439, 446.

Abbott C. J. "Irving & Co., residing in America, had employed the plaintiff residing at Birmingham, to purchase hardware for them in England, by commission. By accepting this employment he became as between him and them their agent. They then send him the bill in question as a further remittance, on account of their order for hardware.

The bill is drawn upon persons residing in London, the plaintiff therefore could not have been expected to present the bill himself; it must have been understood that he was to do this through the medium of some other person. He employed for that purpose, persons in the habit of transacting such business for him and others, and upon whose punctuality he might reasonably rely. In doing this, we think he did all that was incumbent upon him, as between him and Irving & Co., that he is personally in no default as to them and is not answerable to them for the default of the persons whom he employed under such circumstances."

Bromley vs. Coxwell, 2 Bos. & Pull. 438.
Cochran vs. Irlam, 2 M. & Selw. 301 note.
Rapson vs. Cubitt, 9 Mees. & Wels. 710.
Quarman vs. Burnett, 6 Mees. & Wels. 499.
Buckland vs. Conway, 16 Mass. 396.
McMorris vs. Simpson, 21 Wend. 610.

Second—The cases in which it has been decided that a bank receiving a bill or note for collection is liable for any neglect of duty in presenting or giving notice of non-acceptance or non-payment, whether arising from the default of its officers at home, its correspondents abroad, or of agents employed by such correspondents, have no application to this case.

Those cases proceed upon the theory that there is a distinct independent contract or undertaking on the part of the bank to perform the acts necessary for the collection of the paper and not a mere appointment of the bank as an attorney or personal repesentative of the owner of the paper to procure such acts to be done.

Allen vs. Merchants Bank, 22 Wend. 215.
Montgomery County Bank vs. Albany City Bank and Bank of the State of New York, 7 N. Y., (3 Seld,) 459.
Commercial Bank vs. Union Bank, 11 N. Y., (1 Kern) 203.
Ayrault vs. Pacific Bank, 47 N. Y, 570.
Reeves vs. State Bank of Ohio, 8 Ohio St. 465.
Mackesy vs. Ramsays. 9 Clark & Finnelly, 818.

In *Allen vs. Merchants Bank*, Senator Verplanck says "What then is the ordinary *undertaking, contract or agreement* of a bank with one of its dealers in the case of an ordinary deposit of a domestic note or bill payable in the same town received for collection ?

It is a contract made with a corporate body, having only a legal existence, and governed by directors, who can act only by officers and agents.

The *contract* itself is to perform certain duties necessary for the collection of the paper, and the security of the holder. But *neither legal construction nor the common understanding of men of business*, can regard this contract (unless there be some express understanding to that effect,) as an appointment of the bank as an Attorney, or personal representative of the owner of the paper authorized to select other agents for the purpose of collecting the note, and nothing more. There is a wide difference made as well by positive law as by the reason of the thing itself, between a contract, or undertaking to do a thing, and the delegation of an agent or attorney to procure the doing the same thing, between a contract for building a house (for example,) and the appointment of an overseer or superintendent authorized and undertaking to act for the principal in having a house built. * *

It is this distinction on which I have already insisted, as founded on the reason of contracts between *the undertaking to perform anything*, and the mere receiving a delegation of authority to act for another, which reconciles many decisions, &c. * * *

Then the law is clear that by the employment of under agents or servants for his own convenience or to perform part of what he has contracted to do, the employer becomes civilly responsible with those whom he contracts or deals in his business."

The Supreme Court of Ohio in *Reeves vs. The State Bank*, follows the New York cases and adopts both the reasoning and language of Senator Verplanck.

The decisions in *Bradstreet vs. Everson* (72 Penn. St. 124) and *Hoover vs. Wise*, (91 U. S.) (1 Otto) (308), are founded upon the same principles.

In the two cases last mentioned, the collection agency first employed was composed of individuals instead of being a corporation.

In *Bradstreet vs. Everson* the Court held that the receipt for collection imported *an undertaking by the collecting agent himself to collect*, not merely that he received the drafts for transmission to another for collection, for whose negligence he was not to be responsible.

In *Hoover vs. Wise*, Mr. Justice Hunt, who delivered the prevailing opinion, after citing the cases above referred to, says: "We are of the opinion that these authorities fix the rule in the class of cases we are now considering, to-wit, that of attorneys employed not by the creditor, but by a collection agent who *undertakes the collection of the debt*. They establish that such attorney is the agent of the collecting agent and not of the creditor who employed that agent."

In reference to the bank cases cited the learned Justice says: "These cases show that where a bank, as a collection agency, receives a note for the purposes of collection that its position is that of an *independent contractor*, and that the instruments employed by such bank in the business contemplated are its agents, and not the sub-agents of the owner of the note. It is not perceived that it can make any difference that such collection agency is composed of individuals, instead of being an incorporation."

Judge Hunt also cites the case of *Cobb vs. Becke*, (6 Queens Bench, Rep. 930.)

The facts are as follows: Cobb, the plaintiff, was defendant in an action in which one Dally, was his Attorney, and, for the purpose of staying proceedings in that action, he gave to Dally a sum of money sufficient to pay the debt, and costs and requested him to pay it to the plaintiff's Attorney. Dally sent the money to the defendants in the case cited, who were his agents in London, and directed them to pay the debt and costs. They acknowledged receipt of the money, and said it should be applied accordingly, but retained it in satisfaction of a balance due them from Dally.

It was held that there was no privity between the plaintiff and the defendants, and that the action could not be maintained

It was argued that Dally was merely "the hand employed" to forward the money to the defendants, to be by them applied to the payment of the debt and costs.

Lord Denman said that if the facts warranted such a conclusion, doubtless the action might be maintained, but that the facts showed that the plaintiff employed Dally, and that Dally and not the plaintiff employed the defendants.

It would seem that there was clearly an independent undertaking by Dally to pay the debt and costs.

The case at bar is clearly distinguishable from any of the cases cited upon this point.

As has been said the defendant did not contract or undertake to store and take care of the wheat as a warehouseman or bailee.

1st. Such contract cannot be implied from the correspondence between the parties.

The plaintiff in its letter of instructions of September 29th, said: "Please hold above certificates insurance for arrival of vessel, and *on the wheat going into store,* (*i. e.,* into the warehouse of some warehouseman to be selected by you), please have it insured for enough to cover draft On payment of the drafts you will please deliver the cargo (*i. e.,* order the cargo delivered) to order of Messrs. Smith & Co. If not paid please *hold* (*i. e.* hold for us the title or *jus disponendi*) and advise me by telegraph. Messrs. Smith & Co will pay all expenses." Page 18, (fol. 57).

On the 4th October the defendant replied, acknowledging the receipt of the letter and enclosures, and saying: "We prefer, after this, not to receive Bill of Lading when we have to look after the property," (*i. e.* find a warehouse in which it can be stored, make the order for its delivery, procure insurance, &c.) Page 19, (Fol. 58.)

To this letter the plaintiff replied on the 6th October, acknowledging its receipt and saying. "We take very few time cargoes. I would not take any unless we can hold the property. These cargoes were shipped to your bank at the request of Messrs. Smith & Co. and as you wrote me you charged extra for remitting. I supposed it was for the *attention and care requisite.* The usual rate for remitting from Oswego is 1-10 c. On this sight bill you have charged ⅜. On 30th ult. I shipped you another cargo which I trust will receive *your attention.* I shall take no more time cargoes, and in future will not ask you to *look after the property on arrival.*" Page 19, (Fol. 59.)

These letters instead of tending to prove an undertaking by the defendant to store the wheat, are strong evidence to show that neither party supposed that the defendant was assuming any such obligation.

2d. The nature of the transaction, the usage of trade, and the common understanding of men of business are all against the implication of such contract, in this case.

The purpose of the plaintiff in consigning the wheat to the defendant was the protection of its title until the drafts were paid.

The defendant did not employ Smith & Co. for itself, or for its convenience, but for the plaintiff.

The wheat was ordered to the elevator by the defendant and received therein by Smith & Co. expressly *for account of the plaintiff.*

Smith & Co. were neither in law or in fact the agents of the defendant. They were the agents of the plaintiff, and had they received the wheat subject to the usual charges for storage, their claim for such charges would have been against the plaintiff and not against the defendant. So their liability for misconduct or neglect of duty was to the plaintiff and not to the defendant.

Story on Agency, §391, *et seq.,* §§201, 217 *a.*

A privity was created between Smith & Co., and the plaintiff, which did not exist between the principal and the instrument employed by his agent in the cases referred to.

Montgomery Co. Bank vs. Albany City Bank, and Bank of the State of New York. 7 N. Y., (3 Seld.) 459.

Cobb vs. Becke, 6 Q. B. Rep. 930.

Hoover vs Wise, 91 U. S. (1 Otto,) 308.

It has long been the practice of banks to receive bills and notes for collection, and the business of a collection agency is indicated by its title, but the storage of grain has never been or understood to be any part of the business of a bank.

Third. Had the defendant in form contracted with the plaintiff to store and care for the wheat as a warehouseman, such contract would have been *ultra vires*, and would have imposed no legal obligation upon the corporation.

See Second Sub. of Point I.

Fourth. Such contract would have been beyond the scope of the powers of the defendant for any purpose, and therefore it might avail itself of its want of power as a defence to this action.

Miners Ditch Co. vs. Zellerback, 37, Cal. 543, 579.

Selden J. in Bissell vs. the Michigan Southern & Northern Indiana R. R. Co., 22, N. Y., 258, 281.

Talmage vs. Pell, 3 Seld. 328.

Pearce vs. Madison & Indianapolis R. R. Co., and Peru & Indianapolis R. R. Co., 21, How. (U. S.) 441.

McGregor vs. the managers of the Deal & Dover R. R. Co., 16, Eng. Law & Eq. 180.

South Yorkshire R. R. Co. vs. Great Northern R. R. Co., 9 Exch. Rep. 55.

The N. W. Union Packet Co. vs. Shaw, 37, Wis. 655, 19, Am. Rep. 781.

Fifth. The defendant would not be estopped from alleging its want of authority as a defence by the fact that similar contracts had previously been made by its officers.

The repetition of unlawful acts by the officers of a corporation cannot render such acts valid.

> Coleman vs. Eastern Counties Railway Co.,
> 10, Beav. 1.
>
> Bank of Augusta vs. Earle, 13, Peters, 519;
> 587.

III.

The defendant received no portion of the proceeds of the sales of the wheat.

See account of Smith & Co. with defendant. (Pages 39, 40,) and testimony of Mr. DeWolf, the president. (p.59)

The draft of Smith, Wemple & Co. on John Taylor's Sons, mentioned in the account (page 39,) is not the draft paid at the Fourth National Bank, with the fund of Smith & Co., on the 11th October, 1869. (Pages 45, 59.)

They were for different amounts and matured at different times. Besides, it does not appear that any proceeds of the sales of the cargoes of the "Atwater" and "Fort," went to the Fourth National Bank. The reverse seems to be true. (Pages 65, 66.)

The Court below therefore, properly refused to submit to the jury question of the receipt by the defendant, of such proceeds, and to instruct the jury in relation to the payment of the acceptance of John Taylor's Sons as requested by plaintiff's Counsel. Pages 73, (fol. 215,) 74, (fols. 217, 218.)

IV.

Should it be conceded that the defendant assumed the duties and responsibilities of a bailee of the wheat, and was chargeable with fault in ordering the same into the Corn Exchange Elevator, still the plaintiff would not be entitled to recover in this action.

The defendant was not guilty of a conversion of the wheat. The plaintiff found it, took the control of it and dealt with it as its own property, without consulting the defendant, and, if the plaintiff sustained any loss, that loss arose from its own conduct and not from the action of the defendant.

First—The plaintiff found the four boat loads of wheat shipped to Hughes, Hickcox & Co., and John Wilmot, and instead of taking possession of the same, expressly agreed not to replevy it, but to allow it to go into their possession and be sold by them, and rely upon their personal responsibility for its value. (Pages 21, 25, (Fol. 74), 33, 43.)

The plaintiff, by this act, prevented the defendant from regaining possession of the wheat, and it cannot therefore look to the latter for any part of its value.

Story on Agency, §403.

The law imposes upon the party subjected to injury from a breach of contract by another party, the active duty of making reasonable exertions to make the injury as light as possible. And if the injured party through negligence or wilfulness allows the damage to be unnecessarily enhanced the increased loss justly falls on him.

Hamilton vs. McPherson, 28 N. Y., 72.

Shannon vs. Comstock, 21 Wend. 461.

Second—The plaintiff brought actions of trover against Wilmot and Hughes, Hickcox & Co., for these four boat loads of wheat and recovered judgments for the full value of the same. (Pages 21, 33, 42.)

These judgments would have been a bar to actions brought by the defendant against those parties to recover this wheat or the value thereof.

Either the general owner of property or a bailee having a special interest therein, can

4

maintain trover or case for an injury to or conversion of it.

But judgment in an action by the owner is a bar to a suit by the bailee.

"The defendant can never be made liable for the same cause of action to the principal and agent."

Green vs. Clark, 12 N. Y., (2 Kern.) 343.
Story on Agency, §§403, 410.
Brown's Actions at Law, 162.

Third—For ought that appears, both of those judgments were collectable to their full amount.

In the absence of proof the presumption is that they were *Ingalls* vs. *Lord*, 1 Cow. 240; *Allen* vs. *Suydam*, 17 Wend. 368; S. C. 20 Wend. 321, *First Nat. Bank* vs. *Fourth Nat. Bank*, 77 N. Y. 320.

If those judgments were worthless, in whole or in part the plaintiff should have proved it.

The plaintiff will not be permitted to collect the value of its wheat from the parties who converted it to their own use and from this defendant also.

In the language of Earl J. in *First Nat. Bank*, vs. *Fourth Nat. Bank* (p. 330.) *"The plaintiff is entitled to indemnity, and no more for the loss caused by the fault of the defendant, and it must show the extent of such loss."*

Fourth. The plaintiff accepted from Hughes, Hickcox & Co., in satisfaction of the judgment against them a sum considerably less than that due upon it, and settled with Randall & Kenyon, and G. Woolworth, without suit, for the wheat received by them respectively for sums less than the value of such wheat. (Page 42.)

Surely the plaintiff cannot be entitled to recover in this action the sums thus voluntarily relinquished by it.

By making the settlements with Randall and Kenyon and Woolworth, the plaintiff superseded and extinguished the right of the defendant, to obtain redress from them, by suit or otherwise. Story on Agency, §403,

It follows therefore that the plaintiff has sustained no loss from the fault of the defendant, assuming that the defendant was guilty of fault.

V.

Assuming still that the defendant was in fault, the most that the plaintiff would be entitled to recover in this action, would be the amount of the unpaid drafts and the Lake Freight on the wheat.

At the time of the trial, in July, 1877, the amount of the judgments against Hughes, Hickcox & Co., and John Wilmot, exclusive of costs and the sums actually received by the plaintiff from Woolworth and Randall and Kenyon, with interest, together exceeded the amount of the time drafts, and interest and the judgments in the freight suits, paid by the plaintiff with interest, by more than ten thousand dollars.

Judgment against H. H. & Co. July 28th, 1873, $24,865
Interest about,..6,962
Judgment against Wilmot, same date,....................24,658
Interest about,...6,904
Received of Woolworth,...300
Interest,..70
Received of Randall & K...2,473
Interest,...201

       Total,...$66,433
Time drafts, $15,000, $17.000,.............................$32,000
Interest about,..17,172
Freight Judgments, $2,440, $2,040,.......................4,480
Interest,...757

       Total,...$54,409
Difference $12,024.
Pages 42, 18, 43.

VI.

Should it be urged that the defendant, if in fault, was liable for nominal damages, the answer will be that when it is apparent from the whole case that the plaintiff can recover no more than a nominal sum, the court will not grant a new trial though error has been committed. *De minimis non curat lex.*

> McConihe vs. N. Y. and Erie Railroad Co., 20 N. Y., 495.
>
> Hopkins vs. Grinnell, 28 Bark. 533.
>
> Devendorf vs. West, 42 Barb. 227.
>
> Rundell vs. Butler, 10 Wend. 119.

VII.

The objection to the testimony showing the usage of Oswego Banks was properly overruled. (Page 56, Fol. 165.)

See Third Sub. of Point I.

VIII.

The testimony offered by the plaintiff on pages 10–14, (Fol. 38–49;) on pages 62, 63, (Fol. 184–187) and on pages 66–68, (Fol. 195–198,) was properly rejected.

That testimony related to transactions between others than parties to this action of which the defendant had no knowledge and with which it was not connected.

IX.

The testimony offered to show the value of the services and expenses of the attorney in prosecuting the suits against Hughes, Hickcox & Co. and John Wilmot, and in defending the freight cases was properly rejected. Pages 68–70, (Fol. 201, 202, 203. Points I. and II.

X.

The decision that the plaintiff was not entitled to recover the sum paid by it for freight on the cargoes of the "Atwater" and "D. G. Fort" was correct. Page 73, (Fol. 215.)

If the defendant was not liable to the plaintiff for the value of the wheat, it clearly was not liable for the freight.

It may be claimed that the defendant should have made the order for the delivery of the wheat to a warehouseman subject to the payment by A. F. Smith & Co. of the freight.

The defendant was not instructed so to do. On the contrary, the plaintiff wrote: "Messrs. Smith & Co. will pay all expenses."

The defendant was authorized to and did believe that Smith & Co. would pay the freight and so informed the masters of the vessels. Pages 18, (Fol. 57), 45, (Fol. 133) 59, (Fol. 176).

Smith & Co. did attempt to pay the freight. Pages 45–50, 59–61.

XI.

No error was committed by the Court below in its refusal to submit the cause to the jury, or to charge as requested by plaintiff's counsel. Pages 73, 74.

XII.

The judgment of the Circuit Court should be affirmed.

ALBERTUS PERRY,

Attorney, and of Counsel

for Defendant in Error.